6.3

Madness and Modernity

To
Anna Freud

Madness and Modernity

A Study in Social Psychoanalysis

C. R. Badcock

Basil Blackwell

© C.R. Badcock 1983

First published 1983
Basil Blackwell Publisher Limited
108 Cowley Road, Oxford OX4 1JF, England

All rights reserved. No part of this publication may be reproduced, stored in a retrieval system, or transmitted, in any form or by any means, electronic, mechanical, photocopying, recording or otherwise, without the prior permission of the publisher.

Except in the United States of America, this book is sold subject to the condition that it shall not, by way of trade or otherwise, be lent, re-sold, hired out, or otherwise circulated without the publisher's prior consent in any form of binding or cover other than that in which it is published and without a similar condition including this condition being imposed on the subsequent purchaser.

British Library Cataloguing in Publication Data
Badcock, C.R.
Madness and modernity.
1. Social psychology   2. Psychoanalysis
I. Title
302   HM251
ISBN 0-631-12535-3

Typesetting by Oxford Publishing Services, Oxford
Printed in Great Britain
by The Pitman Press Ltd, Bath

Contents

1
The Natural History of the Ego *1*

2
Beyond the Primal Parricide *36*

3
Discontent and its Civilization *62*

4
Group Phylogeny and the Analysis of the Ego *76*

5
The Psychopathology of Present-day Life *89*

6
Art, Externalization and Insight *135*

Bibliography *172*

Index *175*

To tell us that every species of thing is endowed with an occult specific quality by which it acts and produces manifest effects is to tell us nothing; but to derive two or three general principles of motion from phenomena, and afterwards to tell us how the properties and actions of all corporeal things follow from those manifest principles would be a very great step...

Isaac Newton, Optics

1
The Natural History of the Ego

When, in the past, men were confronted with the problem of differentiating themselves from animals they tended to do so in terms of human attributes such as self-consciousness, rationality, free-will, or the possession of a soul or a moral sense. Although such answers may not seem entirely convincing today, principally because of the insights which Darwin and Freud have given us into ourselves, it is nevertheless true that an approach to the problem based on evolution and psychoanalysis would yield analogous, if different, answers. Today, benefiting from psychoanalytic insights, we would probably say that man was distinguishable from the beasts by virtue of his possession of a highly evolved and differentiated ego, and still more by his acquisition of the superego. It is in these agencies of the mind that most of the higher mental functions which are uniquely characteristic of our species occur. Prime examples might be conceptual thought, self-criticism and moral awareness, laughter and, perhaps most essential of all, rational self-consciousness

Yet these ego-structures, although perhaps most distinctive of our species, did not appear whole, complete and without a past. Like just about everything, they had a history and, like most other phenomena based on biological processes — for the ego and superego, although purely psychological agencies, nevertheless require a brain in which to function — evolved over an extended period of time. The evolution of human ego-structures is of immense significance not only for psychoanalytic ego-psychology but also for the principal subject of this book: namely, the psychopathology of our times and its relation to the cultural, economic and psychological evolution of our species. Let us begin then with a brief review of what we know about the ego's past in order all the better to be able to understand something about its present and future.

I shall begin by concentrating on the ego, which may be defined as an agency of the personality differentiated from the wholly unconscious id by its responsibilities for the control of voluntary movement. In this sense it is first and foremost the executive agency of the mind and is charged with the fundamental functions of decision-making and surveillance of the input from the senses as well as sensations arising from the instinctual drives of the id.

In this rather basic definition — which, be it noted, makes no reference to self-consciousness as such — the ego is clearly not uniquely human. Whilst one may argue that it would be wrong to attribute ego-functions to animals in which the id/ego differentiation was difficult to justify because their behaviour was largely under instinctual, pre-programmed control, it is nevertheless true that some mammals — and in particular some higher primates — do seem to show a plasticity of behaviour and an elaboration of activity which clearly point to the beginnings, however primitive, of ego-functions proper. The chief candidates for this distinction are most certainly the higher primates, and of them perhaps more especially the near relatives of man, the chimpanzee and gorilla. In the case of these species, rigidly determined, genetically programmed instinctual behaviour has given way to much less clearly focused instinctual drives.

A striking example of this tendency for instinct to diffuse into drive is seen in the sexual behaviour of the chimpanzee. In the past great difficulty was encountered in persuading chimpanzees raised in zoos to mate successfully. It was found that males and females would become sexually excited and were strongly motivated to mate even though they seemed incapable of correctly carrying out the act of copulation. The female when on heat was obviously erotically inclined herself, and could soon arouse the male, but, once aroused, the sexual drive of both animals seemed unable to direct them towards the exact behaviour demanded by the situation. However, chimpanzees raised in the wild seemed to have no such difficulties, presumably because they had had plenty of opportunity to observe copulation in other chimpanzees and so had learnt how to perform it themselves. Similar observations seem to apply to another type of basic behaviour which is in most other animals under direct genetic control, namely, care of the young. Here again, higher primates in captivity seem to be motivated in the right general direction, but appear to need some element of learning to be able to focus the instinctual drive towards its goal.

What is true of the chimpanzee and the higher primates in general is even more true of man. In our species rigidly set behavioural patterns for social or sexual behaviour do not exist. The neurological dominance of the large human cerebral cortex has ensured that basic instinct has come increasingly under its control and has thereby lost its specific and rigidly determined character. This of course, is the explanation of the immense variability, imaginativeness, and adaptability of human behaviour, and it is also obviously the basis of the evolution of the ego.

It seems that in the case of the higher primates the diffusion and decay of specific instinctual behaviours has facilitated — perhaps even necessitated — the evolution of a primitive and elementary ego-organization, that is, one in which unfocused instinctual drives are increasingly brought under the control of the higher cortical centres which facilitate drive-management and decision-making on the basis of great adaptive flexibility of response. Such flexibility of response is obviously the basis of intelligence, but also, as the earlier example of the mating problems of captive chimpanzees shows, the foundation of the instinctual lability which can lead to perversion, inhibition and, in man at least, to neurosis, insanity and civilization.[1]

If we enquire into the evolutionary background to this situation, it is immediately clear that the evolution of behaviour in both humans and primates rests on a common mammalian basis which can doubtless be traced to the greater adaptiveness, activity and independence of environmental conditions which the acquisition of warm-bloodedness provided. The fact that mammals have, by and large, relatively bigger brains and higher intelligence than most reptiles already points towards the evolutionary trend which reaches its culmination in man and which substitutes elaborated patterns of learned and intelligent behaviour for simple instinctual response with automatic, stereotyped actions. Not only the continuous activity of the mammal, by contrast to the general torpor and intermittent liveliness of the reptile, but also the wider range of its behaviour and its ecological adaptation call for a more plastic, adaptable behavioural response.

In the primates this trend has been continued, probably not leased because, having been tree-dwellers and still being predominantly arboreal, the primates have developed a much greater reliance on vision and a correspondingly lesser reliance on the sense of smell. The significance of this is that not merely does sight — particularly the excellent stereoscopic colour vision of the

---

[1] K. R. Eissler, 'The fall of man', *Psychoanalytic Study of the Child*, XXX, p. 596.

primates — require a developed cerebral cortex, but it also tends to mean progressive emancipation from the basic chemical and pheromonal control of behaviour seen in many mammals in which the sense of smell has retained its pristine importance. The captive chimpanzee would have no difficulty with mating if its mating behaviour — like that of a great many mammals — were simply triggered by the sense of smell and by hormonal or pheromonal stimulation. But, in a situation in which an arboreal habitat has led to a reliance on visual cues and a generalized body-structure and postural suppleness, even the correct mating-position may not be obvious and automatic as it is in many other animals.

Perhaps the clearest example of the way in which the arboreal adaptations of the ancestral primates has resulted in opportunities for the evolution of adaptable and intelligent behaviour is the case of the primate hand. This organ, like the ancestral primate foot, evolved the capacity of prehensility — that is, the ability to grasp things — originally, obviously, branches. Yet the primate hand, particularly in the case of man, who has retained (or, more accurately, re-acquired) a generalized, unspecialized hand, can be put to many other uses than merely grasping branches. If some measure of upright posture is possible the hand, originally evolved to hold on to trees, can also be used to hold on to sticks, stones, tools and artefacts. It possesses a wealth of adaptive possibilities which only required the evolution of an adaptive, intelligent brain to be realized. In the higher primates these possibilities can already be seen emerging as actualities when chimpanzees use twigs to get at the occupants of a termite-mound, or wave branches to scare off leopards. Such behaviours as these require the development of the basic ego-function of drive-inhibition and re-direction — the suppression of an obvious, instinctual response in favour of an indirect, but intelligent one. Thus when the chimpanzee, supplied in the laboratory with two boxes and a stick to reach a suspended bunch of bananas, stops leaping up and trying the reach them with its hands and instead puts one box on top of the other, climbs up and dislodges the bananas with the stick, it is using to the full its basic ability to suppress the automatic response — leaping up — in favour of the intelligent one — climbing up and reaching with the stick. Such an achievement is the exact contrary of the plight of the captive chimpanzee who cannot discover how to copulate. In this case, cerebral development has denied it the automatic response while defective social development has denied it the opportunity of learning the skill it lacks. As we shall see quite shortly, cerebral development, ego-evolution and socialization are all closely related phenomena, above all in man, and in modern man no less than in his ancestors.

Yet it would be wrong, in the course of this rather general discussion, to make the common mistake of ignoring the contribution which basic instinctual drives themselves make to such adaptive, intelligent behaviour. The chimpanzee in the laboratory would be unlikely to solve the box-stick-and-banana problem if it had no initial interest in the bananas. Indeed, experimenters have found — not suprisingly — that a hungry chimpanzee is more likely to find the solution than a satiated one. Here, instinctual need provides the impetus for intelligent action, and an instinctual drive which would merely make a hungry dog bark at a suspended bone makes a hungry primate build, climb and reach with a tool. It is a commonplace to see culture as man's building, climbing and reaching — indeed, one whole school of anthropology sees it as his tool-making — but it is important not to forget that in man, as in the other primates, intelligent, adaptive behaviour — behaviour, in other words, mediated by the ego — is motivated by his instinctual drives. Indeed, if we fail to take such drives into account we shall fail more or less totally in accounting for his behaviour, and certainly in explaining its evolution. We would run the risk, commonly seen in most discussions of this kind, of reducing the most interesting, revealing and profound insight into the basis of human behaviour to vague platitudes and banal — if irrefutable — generalizations. On the other hand, if we ignore the ego and its functions in man and concentrate on his instincts as if they could totally account for his behaviour as they do in animals who lack an ego, we should fall into the alternative trap of failing to account for his culture at all except as the outcome of doubtful instinctual behaviour of an altruistic or civilized kind. The situation is clearly a complex one, with instinctual drives of a diffuse, unfocused nature being directed and controlled by higher mental functions of the ego-organization. To account for this we need to take seriously both sides of the picture: the instinctual one and the psychological, cultural one.

Specifically, this means not only taking into account man's obvious close evolutionary ties with the chimpanzee and gorilla, but also his rather less obvious resemblance to another primate, the gelada baboon. For the fact of the matter is that we shall be misled if, along with most other enquiries in this field to date, we perhaps rather naively imagine that if man's earliest ego is found preserved, as it were, in the chimpanzee, then there we shall also find the evolutionary basis of his id. As we shall now see, this is not at all the case.

By id in this context I mean the unconscious, instinctual basis of behaviour from which man's ego has become differentiated. This is not an exact equivalent of the meaning of the term in Freud's writings and in psychoanalysis subsequently, but it will serve as a starting-point for our investigation of the specific determinants of human psychology. By comparison with the highly organized and elaborately structured ego, Freud characterized the id as chaotic,[2] even though in practice he attributed to it a definite and distinguishable shape. He may never have envisioned a situation in which it would be possible to specify in some detail the characteristics of the phylogenetic id, the evolutionary starting-point from which the modern id–ego organization began. Yet this is exactly what we are now able to do, thanks to our present understanding of human evolution and in particular to the theory which explains the evolutionary acquisitions of man since he parted company with the ancestors of today's great apes.

Let me take as a telling example the facts regarding human sexual dimorphism. Most primates are sexually dimorphic — in other words, the sexes differ from one another in certain regular physical characteristics. There is notable sexual dimorphism, for instance, in man's close evolutionary relative, the chimpanzee, and even more in the gorilla. But man is, in general, sexually dimorphic in ways which do not resemble his ape cousins. For instance, man — or perhaps here I should say *men* — lack the huge canine teeth which distinguish the male great apes. Admittedly, there is a general difference in body-build and size between men and women, and this is analogous to sexual dimorphism in the simians, but man's most distinctive secondary sexual characteristics are quite unlike anything found in the gorilla or chimpanzee. They are, however, closely comparable to what we find in the gelada baboon. Here, we encounter the same pattern which so clearly distinguishes man from the apes — notable absence of canine-tooth dimorphism, prominent displays of hair

---

[2] Sigmund Freud, *New Introductory Lectures on Psychoanalysis*, XXII, p. 73. This, and all other references to the works of Freud, is from *The Standard Edition of the Complete Psychological Works of Sigmund Freud*, by volume and page number.

around the face and neck of the male and, in the female, a secondary sexual display on the chest.

The explanation of this remarkable correspondence between patterns of sexual dimorphism in humans and gelada baboons it to be found in evidence of parallels in the evolution of the two species which have been attributed to the likely existence of our hominid ancestors in a habitat similar to that of today's gelada baboon and to a resultant comparability of life-style and evolutionary adaptation. This theory, first advanced by Clifford Jolly[3] and described by myself at greater length elsewhere,[4] enables us to draw detailed conclusions regarding the instinctual repertoire of our pre-human ancestors.

Let us take the example of sexual dimorphism once again. The absence of simian sexual dimorphism affecting canine-tooth development, cranial crests and so on in males might lead us to conclude that man was not endowed originally with instinctual dispositions of a sexual kind comparable to those of the modern great apes. Yet his possession of patterns of sexual dimorphism closely comparable to those of the modern gelada baboon point with equal force to the supposition that modern man acquired along with those gross features of bodily structure behavioural propensities appropriate to them. This has been overwhelmingly borne out by clinical psychoanalytic investigations of the id. Gelada sexual dimorphism is only a part of a larger adaptive complex based on the fact that these baboons live in small groups in savanna grasslands subsisting on a diet of vegetable matter, presumably much as our hominid ancestors did. Such a mode of subsistence demands that the population be relatively sparsely dispersed, at least during the daytime while foraging is

---

[3] C. Jolly, 'The seed-eaters: a new model of hominid differentiation based on a baboon analogy', *Man*, 5 (1), 1970.
[4] C. Badcock, *The Psychoanalysis of Culture*, Oxford, 1980, pp. 6–8.

going on. Since the important variable in population size is always the number of females rather than the number of males (because one male can impregnate a large number of females but any female can only manage one pregnancy at a time), selective forces determine that the daytime gelada social structure is one in which a single dominant male forages with an attendant group of females and young. Sexually mature males are driven out of this group once they grow big enough to constitute a threat to the dominant male (although occasionally an ageing dominant male will allow a younger male to take over his harem and will be tolerated by his successor for a while). Younger males who have no harems also form groups without young or females, and so effectively there are two kinds of group: the one-male group and the multi-male group. In this situation it is obvious why notable sexual dimorphism exists among gelada and similar open-country baboons. The reason is that all males are potential — and usually actual — competitors for females; hence sexual selection favours males who optimize male characteristics. From the behavioural point of view, the principal male characteristic is sadistic sexual egoism, since is it clear that only the male who is capable of driving off his rivals can hold on to the females of the breeding group. (This is true even when the successor to a dominant male is one who was an accepted heir-apparent. He too must drive off rivals once his older patron is gone if he is to remain in possession of his inherited females.) In gelada-like populations selection will favour males who are most successfully competitive with other males for ownership of females and young.

Such behavioural propensities to egoism, sexual rivalry and authoritarian domination of the family group are in stark contrast to what we normally regard as civilized, human behaviour. Our laws, taboos and standards of conduct normally forbid sons to fight each other and their fathers for exclusive possession of the women of the family. Yet this is exactly the behavioural propensity of the id uncovered by clinical psychoanalysis. Over and over again, in all cultures, psychoanalytic investigations insistently reveal what Freud termed the 'Oedipus complex' but what we might with equal justice call the 'Gelada complex'.[5]

In short, the phylogenetic basis of the id seems most definitely to be a set of basically egoistic and anti-social sexual and aggressive drives which cause all men to see each other as sexual rivals and which make sons desire the death of their fathers for possession of the mother and sisters. (Even the gelada heir-apparent phenomenon, when it exists, cannot get away from this, any more than the human heir-apparent can fail to look forward to the demise of his patron who, to this extent, is also his rival.) Thus the crime of Oedipus — murder of the father, mating with the mother — is really nothing more than what comes naturally to the gelada male, and, I think, to our hominid ancestors who, when they acquired numerous gelada-like physical adaptations, must also have acquired the appropriate behavioural responses and instinctual drives. (As far as modern women are concerned, an analogous situation must exist in which the demands of civilization — principally incest-avoidance and respect for the paternal authority — represent a recent and indeed onerous imposition on an earlier instinctual nexus which knew nothing of this, indeed which perhaps was the foundation of that submissiveness to male aggressiveness which still seems to underlie the female sexual constitution. For example, the modern female hostage who falls in love with her captor may not merely be manifesting the well-known defence of 'identification with

---

[5] For refutation of the myth that the Oedipus complex is culture-bound see the works of G. Roheim, esp. *Psychoanalysis and Anthropology*, New York, 1950.

the aggressor' (particularly since it is not so much identification with him as submission to him), she may instead be giving way to her phylogenetic id and its demand that a female captured by a male should look to him for sexual satisfaction. (In the case of the hamadryas baboon — a species closely comparable to the gelada in adaptations and sociobiology — the female instinctively runs *towards* the male when barked at.))

However, the relevance of the foregoing theory of hominid evolution does not apply only to secondary sexual characteristics and to the structure of the id. It is also vitally relevant to the evolution of the ego and superego.

One consequence of subsistence on a gelada-like diet is that, as Jolly puts it, 'a chewing apparatus of the hominid type might be expected to include a thick, muscular, mobile tongue, accommodated in a large oral cavity . . . also, incidentally, providing preadaptations to articulate speech.'[6] The significance of language for the later development of the ego can hardly be underestimated; indeed, there is little doubt that, had articulate speech not evolved, modern ego-functions would not have developed as they did and self-awareness, rational thought and social evolution would all have been greatly inhibited in their development in our species. It is clear that, on the most fundamental level, the ability to substitute a thought conveyed in linguistic terms for an action or a thing is an absolutely basic ingredient of the ego's functioning: it is the key to the ego's ability to distance itself from the immediate demands of the id and its drives and to evolve higher, more abstract thought-processes than those available to an animal, no matter how intelligent, which lacks the power of speech. Furthermore, we should recall that in

[6] 'The seed-eaters', p. 18.

modern individuals (and almost certainly also in the past) internalized verbal commands and prohibitions are of the first significance in the acquisition of the superego and manifest this aspect of themselves in the auditory hallucinations of accusing and scorning voices so often found in paranoia.

Again, referring to the possible origin of our upright posture, Jolly remarks that 'locomotion of any kind is infrequent during gelada-like foraging, so that . . . it is an ideal apprenticeship for an adapting biped.'[7]

In conjunction with considerable manual dexterity derived in part from the ability to oppose thumb and index finger which man shares with the gelada baboon and presumably derives from the same source (picking up small objects of the diet), the adoption of an upright posture created the right conditions for the final emancipation of the hand from locomotion and set man on the path which led to the invention and use of tools and to material culture in general. But even more important than this is the psychological significance of such a development. The ego is, as we have seen, principally the executive agency of the personality and has as its most characteristic attribute control of voluntary movement. The final emancipation of the hand from locomotion and its refined dexterity in handling small objects presented the evolving ego with its greatest opportunity and with its greatest challenge where direction of the manual musculature was concerned. Now that the hand was not naturally and exactly adapted for one specific task it became generally adaptable for just about everything and hence the agency which ultimately controlled the hand was now called on to give it the directions which automatic instinct and locomotive reflexes no longer could. The hand now became the general factotum of its master, the ego, and the ego, faced with this new

---

[7] *Ibid.*, p. 19.

responsibility for directing an all-purpose organ of gesture and general dexterity, was now further promoted in the psychological economy over the unconscious, automatic and reflexive id. (Part of the reason for this undoubtedly lay in the fact that the foraging hominids of whom we are speaking were in part already pre-adapted to upright posture by an evolutionary past different to that of today's gelada baboon[8] and because they probably already possessed cerebral development going beyond that of a mere monkey thanks to their common ancestry with today's great apes.)

If we recall what was said earlier regarding the trend in primate evolution which promoted the visual sense over that of smell and prehensile agility over terrestrial quadrupedalism, we can readily see that the definitive adoption of a fully upright posture in man is only the culmination of this much more general evolutionary tendency. But in the light of what has been said we can also see that it was of especial significance in emancipating, not merely the hand from locomotion, but the brain from its reliance on chemical stimuli mediated by the sense of smell. So important is this factor in shaping the evolution of man that Freud, in a number of places in his works,[9] but principally in a footnote to *Civilization and its Discontents*, comments at length on the way in which the adoption of an erect posture in man produced what he termed an 'organic repression' which paved the way for civilization.[10] We can now not only see how justified this comment was but, in details inaccessible to Freud at the time he was writing, can determine with some exactness both the causes and the consequences of this fateful development in human evolution. Basically, it reduces to the realization that man's gelada-

---

[8] *Ibid.*
[9] I, pp. 268–9; X, p. 248; XI, p. 189.
[10] XXI, p. 100n.

like past — which must have lasted for a very considerable period, even by the standards of evolutionary time — left an indelible stamp on both his id and his ego. On the id our gelada — like foraging career left instinctual trends which far from favouring altruism, strongly motivated males to sadistic sexual egoism and perhaps correspondingly imprinted on females a fatalistic, passive tendency which Freud was to term 'feminine masochism'.[11] On the ego it left a stamp which definitively brought about in man the culmination of the long primate evolutionary trend towards dominance of the higher cortical centres over the lower, olfactory ones, and the final emancipation of his fore-limb from locomotion and of his responses from direct chemical stimuli. With the first of these emancipations went the opportunity to create his material and technological culture; with the second, comparable opportunities for his mental and social culture.

If we now enquire into what exactly the acquisition of a fully upright posture and all its attendant psychological advantages had for our hominid ancestors I think that we are now in a position to give a fairly specific and detailed answer. Put in the baldest terms, one can say that the result of all this was that man — or, perhaps I should say, the hominid ancestors of modern man — became able to hunt, and that, with the success of the hunting economy, came culture and civilization as we know it and with it its psychological corollary: the superego.

Elsewhere,[12] I have elaborated at length on the reasons why it is implausible to suggest that the first hunters were the ruling males of what Freud termed the 'primal hordes', but rather the unmated, younger males of the all-male

---

[11] 'The economic problem of masochism', XIX p. 161.
[12] *The Psychoanalysis of Culture*, pp. 9–11.

groups, Freud's 'sons'. Summarizing the argument, let me say that there are good reasons, based on sociobiological insights into hunting, which lead me to suppose that the cooperation, altruism and mutuality demanded by social-hunting techniques in 4-foot high hominids lacking all modern hunting technology meant that only the sons were likely at first to start to exploit the immense reserves of game which our gelada-like ancestors saw all around them on the savanna grasslands where they lived. Furthermore, one might point out that modern observations of innovation in primate behaviour — particularly with regard to feeding techniques — shows that it is always the younger animals who are the experimenters.

My theory therefore suggests that bands of young male hominids started to hunt first, while older, dominant males, encumbered with their harems and young, continued the traditional foraging. What this meant in practical terms was that the hunters were non-reproductive, and presumably in order to become reproductive had to give up their youthful way of life and return to the traditional mode of subsistence. However, once a hunting group acquired females and retained its cooperative, more egalitarian social structure, immense benefits in terms of natural selection would follow mainly because survival — and therefore evolutionary fitness — would be greatly enhanced for all, in contrast to the previous foraging way of life with its great limitations on mutual support, its dietary individualism, lack of home-bases, poor nutrition and so on.

The problem, in terms of the present discussion, is to explain how the evolution of the id and the ego up to the point at which hunting began could have resulted in its success and could have brought about the adaptive advance represented by self-reproducing hunting bands. The answer to the problem is to be found in the Freudian concept of the *superego*.

The Natural History of the Ego

So far there has been little discussion of the superego for the simple reason that there has been little cause to mention it. In the remote period of human history which we have been discussing it simply did not exist. The superego is a relatively modern acquisition and is the psychological agency which is the inner counterpart of what in the outer world we would call 'culture' or 'civilization'. It is a part of the ego-organization, and developed out of it in some ways rather as the ego itself differentiated from the id. In modern clinical psychoanalysis it manifests itself as that part of the ego which represents a critical self-awareness which is both censorious and exhortatory, being the representative of standards, ideals, commands and prohibitions. In the individual it is largely modelled on the parents — normally most particularly on the parent of the same sex — and in the species derives from the collective parent — the father of the primal horde.

To understand why this is so let us recapitulate for a moment. We have established that our hominid ancestors in their gelada-like stage of evolution had acquired an aggressive, egoistic id (sadistic in males, masochistic in females), along with the beginnings of an ego which had at its disposal the powerful, but relatively unfocused instinctual drives of the id, and rudimentary, but real capabilities for their inhibition, redirection, and inventive deployment in novel, even intelligent forms of behaviour. This behavioural plasticity and mental agility, optimized as always in the young, began sooner or later to express itself in a new mode of subsistence, namely, hunting. This was quintessentially a redirection, redeployment and adaptation of the id, for hunting is self-evidently a highly aggressive and instinctually satisfying occupation (which is presumably why it has been retained as a sport in more evolved societies). Yet, as I have already said, the hunting of our hominid ancestors had to be communal.

This apparently insignificant detail was to be of fateful

importance for all subsequent human cultural and psychological evolution because it provided the first, albeit rather minimal, check on the egoism and mutual antagonism of males. Today we take it for granted that such antagonism must be inhibited in a civilized society and we have developed all sorts of cultural and social institutions to procure such inhibitions in the form of religious, moral and legal prohibitions backed up by agencies of social control and law-enforcement. But, in the beginning, such checks did not exist. On the contrary, as we have seen, in a gelada-like existence they are inappropriate. There the only check on egoism and intra-group antagonism is the superior egoism and antagonism of its head, the dominant male. Of course, in the all-male groups — the sons — things were a little better. Because these groups did not include females there was no reason why individual males should fight one another for their possession and exploitation. Consequently, as in all-male groups in modern gelada populations, we would expect to find much less in the way of mutual antagonism and more in the way of sociability and cooperation. This sociability and cooperation lent itself ideally to communal hunting techniques because, as I have shown elsewhere,[13] hunting success, even among well-adapted hunting animals — which, of course, our hominid ancestors most decidedly were not — is generally proportional to the number of hunters involved.

The mutuality and cooperativeness of the first hunting bands were also in part probably the outcome of the fact that the hunted quarry was not a member of their own species and, as such, the hunt would have been a crucial example of our species' natural and very considerable aggression being directed away from fellow hominids on to animals. Yet, if such all-male groups were to reproduce

---

[13] *Ibid.*, p. 10.

themselves as hunting groups and gain the immense adaptive advantages that situation bestowed, they would have had to institute at least one, and probably several, hunts against members of their own species — the primal fathers who, of course, monopolized all the females. In his *Totem and Taboo* Freud made such an act of primal parricide and rape the origin of all subsequent human culture. This was because, for him, it was the origin of the superego. To see why this is so let us consider the situation in the light of the foregoing argument.

Essentially, what had to happen was that a group of adolescent males without females had to obtain some, without allowing their group to dissolve in internecine strife over who would become the owner of the newly acquired females. Yet, if they were all to own them, some mechanism would have to emerge to inhibit their natural sexual rivalry. This mechanism was the superego.

Effectively, it boiled down to a continuation in a certain sense of the original situation, except that now the primal father exercised his authority not in the social group, but within the ego — he became a psychological agency instead of being a physical reality. But what brought about this remarkable transformation? For, as we shall see, it is a remarkable and essential transformation, one which occurred at the beginning of human culture but which, in some subsequent cultures — possibly even in the modern world — could undergo retransformation back again into what it originally had been — an external tyranny. The question really is this: how does external coercion and imposed altruism become internal self-control and restraint?

An initial answer might be: by means of *identification*. Identification is a process which occurs when the ego, in part abandoning its awareness of itself as a separate entity, equates itself, or some aspect of itself, with some external thing. In the case which we are examining, that external thing was the dominant male member of the reproductive group of the foraging hominids — Freud's primal father. Even before hunting began, his sons would have had cause to identify with him because each and every one of them was powerfully motivated by the drives of his id to wish to become such a primal father in his turn. But such an identification was probably more than merely an exercise in wish-fulfilment by the ego on behalf of the id. It was also probably in part a defensive measure on the part of the ego itself.

Today, a well-known, but primitive, type of ego-defence exists, termed *identification with the aggressor*. Typically, it consists in an attempt to ward off criticism or some other kind of attack on the part of an authority-figure by means of exchanging subject for object and thus putting the recipient of the attack in the place of the attacker. A little girl described by Anna Freud got over her anxiety about seeing ghosts in the dark hall of her home by advising her brother, 'There's no need to be afraid in the hall. You just have to pretend that you're the ghost who might meet you.'[14]

Such a reaction is closely analogous to one frequently observed among baboons and other primates. Here, if one animal is attacked by another above it in the status-hierarchy, the attacked animal, rather than fighting back, instead directs its aggression against some inferior — a means of dealing with the situation which is open to all except the most subordinate member of the group.

A comparable reaction to the sadistic tyranny of the primal fathers would have been natural to the sons. It would have served as a substitute-gratification for their own sadism (i.e., 'I cannot retaliate against my father, but I can against my younger brother'); but also as a defence on the part of the ego (i.e., 'I am spared the anxiety of

[14] *The Ego and the Mechanisms of Defence* London, 1968, p. 111.

being made the object of an attack if I can instead become the attacker'); finally, it would also have contributed a first, rudimentary focus for the superego (i.e., 'My father is not now the attacker — I am — hence I am to that extent my father!').

We can be fairly certain that such a reaction did occur, not merely because it is observable among modern primates, but because it had to exist if young males were, in due course of time, to supplant the fathers, and this, for the purposes of reproduction, they had to do. Hence selective forces would have favoured the most successful at doing it. Furthermore, it is probable that identification with the aggressor still exists today in young children or those with regressed or fixated ego-development for this very reason: namely, that it has become a part of the genetically inherited behavioural repertoire of our species.

Yet identification with the aggressor, even if it may suggest a very early and rudimentary phase in superego development and therefore in internalization of the primal father, cannot explain what had to happen next; for, as we have seen, the crucial turning-point would have come only when aggression within the brother-band became inhibited. For this to happen, aggressive drives, directed away from the father on to others in the manner which we have just described, would have had to become internalized also and turned, not against some other, but back against the self.

The specific mechanism suggested by Freud in *Totem and Taboo* (and corroborated by my own research), is that of the murder of the primal father by his sons — or, at least, by those whose egos were sufficiently evolved to experience the considerable distortion caused by their ambivalence regarding him. Ambivalence means that they both loved, admired, revered and desired to emulate him while simultaneously hating and fearing him and wishing to be rid of him. For the id, of course, such contradictory feelings pose no problem; they are natural to it. This is a manifestation of what Freud meant by the chaos of the id — the fact that it can contain within itself contradictory and mutually excluding instinctual drives without ever registering any distortion. But for the ego, things are quite different. A managerial agency — *any* managerial agency, be it psychological or otherwise — cannot cope easily with contradictory demands and impulses if it is responsible for a choice of action and must take into account the limitations of the real world. The ego knows that if it has to make choices in the world of actuality it cannot keep its cake and eat it too; the id does not. Thus the ego is distorted and disturbed by ambivalence, while the id is oblivious of it.

Because the sons of the primal father both loved and hated him the possibility arose that those of them who by luck or design chanced on their actual fathers in their hunt for women and killed him or drove him off (most probably the former, the latter seems insufficiently traumatic) would have gratified one side of their ambivalent feelings, but would by the same action have frustrated the other. With the primal father dead and gone, and the act of rape of the mothers and sisters consummated, the positive side of the ambivalence got the upper hand and the ego, now relieved of an inner conflict by satisfaction of one of two contradictory desires, could allow itself to gratify the one which remained, namely, love for, and obedience to the father. Now, under the impact of guilt and remorse motivated by the positive side of the original ambivalent feelings for the father, the ego sought to defend itself from further conflict with its id by erecting safety measures which would protect it from such distorting and stressful impulses. It adopted the prohibitions actually enforced by the primal father while he was alive in the form of collective neurotic prohibitions (taboos) now that he was dead.

The prohibitions in question were those against parricide and incest; but of these that against incest had priority because it was the occasion for the temptation to commit the latter. The defence thus utilized one side of the ambivalence — the love and high esteem felt for the father — to build a bulwark against the other — the hate and contempt of the father — in order to inhibit the aggressive egoism of males and make them all equally subject to a primal father-figure who for the first time now became fully internalized as a shared superego. Such sharing of the superego constitutes what we call religion; and the particular religious form which he assumed was that of the animal totem, a choice appropriate in the new hunting culture and a consequence of the fact that the primal father had been the last of the truly animal hominids. From now on, hominids were human. They were human because they possessed the essentials of the superego and with it the genuinely human phenomena of culture, religion and neurosis. Indeed, their culture was a neurosis — a collective animal phobia in which the totem-animal became the psychological reincarnation of the fearsome primal father. This was why he was feared and tabooed as the totem, but this was also why he was periodically sacrificed and consumed by the clan brothers in rituals which re-enacted the primal trauma and the occasion of his first emergence as a psychological force of self-restraint.

It seems probable that all of this could not have come about had not the superego emerged as a continuation of a trend of evolutionary development which had long since been embarked upon by the ego proper. As I pointed out above, the essence of the ego's operations was its ability to redeploy and redirect the malleable drives of the id. The emergence of the superego vastly extended this trend because it represented a characteristically human — or, we might say, neurotic — tendency: namely, an ability to redirect a drive to the extent that it is turned back against the ego itself (i.e., hate of the father becomes hate of oneself for hating him). The consequence of turning an aggressive, egoistic drive back against the self in this characteristic way was to turn egoism into altruism, and agression into self-punishment and guilt. Now the sons, dominated by their love for and estimation of the primal father could maintain the altruism and cooperativeness of their way of life because of their guilt regarding the one thing that had always threatened that cooperation — their lust. The overriding sexual prohibitions of primal hunting societies, expressed today in the complex marriage-rules, kinship-systems and incest-prohibitions of aboriginal peoples, attests to the fundamental necessity of containing the mutual sexual antagonism of males in societies where social cooperation has become the fundamental basis of culture and in which internalization of the collective superego effects this more efficiently than external coercion.

Up to this point I have described these complex psychological developments in a manner which has attempted to make them as clear and as intelligible as possible. Yet it is important to realize that they were neither intelligible nor clear to those in whose minds they actually occurred. It is essential to realize that, far from being consciously understood with insight into their inner meaning, all of these psychological developments were totally unconscious and accompanied by no insight whatsoever.

The reasons for this are easily seen. First, there is the consideration that we are dealing with a phase of human ego-evolution in which language probably barely existed at all and in which a sophisticated awareness of inner conflicts — what today we would call insight — could barely have existed either (indeed, as we shall see later on, it is doubtful to what extent it exists even today!). Secondly, we must recall that the mental conflicts which I am identifying as the origins of human society and civilized behaviour — essentially those portrayed in the story of Oedipus — were as intensely painful and unpleasurable to those who experienced them then as they are to those who experience them in our own times. I have already explained why it is, for instance, that ambivalence, while being no real problem for the id, is a stressful conflict for the ego. If such unpleasurable, stressful psychological conflicts develop, the ego, as part of its defensive strategy, employs a characteristic method of getting rid of them — it *represses* them.

Repression is self-evidently a defensive procedure, designed to obliterate any trace of the repressed material and to safeguard against its return. Clearly, then, if human sociability is based, not on social instincts as such, but on the inhibition, redirection and sublimation of anti-social instinctual drives, it is obvious why these redirecting, inhibiting and sublimating mechanisms must be shielded from conscious thought and further interference. A creature like man, completely lacking the inbred altruism seen, for instance, in the worker bee, might well rebel against the altruistic demands of his society if it were readily apparent to him that his altruism was profoundly hypocritical and made up of components of inhibited egoism, self-directed sadism (e.g. guilt) and de-sexualized libido (e.g. 'social feeling'). Indeed, the very property of being conscious might undo the force of these arrangements since it is the characteristic of conscious thought to change, work-over and constantly review its operations against the datum of the senses and the inner needs of the organism. As is unhappily all too apparent to the student of human nature, purely conscious intentions, even when whole-heartedly adhered to, are ready subject matter for forgetting, for mistakes, or for plain abandonment the moment something more interesting or more desirable comes along. Such observations, however, are not true of the unconscious. Here, insulated by repression from direct awareness, mental representations can live on unsuspected and unknown. Like a city buried by a volcano, they remain frozen in time, untouched by the change, decay and renewal which constantly alter the structures of our conscious mental life.

This has been the fate of the foundation of human sociability — they have been comprehensively repressed, because if they had not been then the conflict between man's instinctual drives and his social existence would have been even more painful and even more disruptive than it is. Indeed, it is doubtful if, but for the forces of repression, the higher social life of the human species could ever have become what it has.

To put the matter another way, we might say that the beginnings of humans society were *traumatic* — that is, that they were occasioned by an overwhelmingly powerful and unexpected event for which our ancestors were not prepared by any instinctual responses of an automatic sort and which left long-lasting and indeed indelible effects on the human psyche. Because the change to a hunting society was, in evolutionary terms, a sudden one and because the human id was not adapted for it (on the contrary, the id was, and has remained, that of a gelada-like forager) only drastic changes in the ego — and in particular the emergence of the superego — could deal with it. It seems that the traumatic events surrounding the over-throw of the primal hordes and the setting up of the first fraternal hunting clans produced in our ancestors a central psychological conflict of such huge and all-engulfing proportions that all subsequent generations have to some extent or other felt its effects. Unable fully to abreact their responses to the trauma in their still quite limited conscious awareness, and unprepared by evolution for the revolutionary change which had suddenly overtaken them, our distant hominid ancestors dealt with the upheaval in their psychological and social lives in part by repressing it and forcing out of consciousness the irreconcilable conflicts which now occupied their instinctual drives. In doing so they bequeathed to all subsequent generations a psychology flawed by conflict and neuroticism and a social life marred by incompatible interests and painful compromises.

But these considerations which, as we shall see later in this book, are of the utmost significance for our principal theme, also touch on a paradox to which the reader's attention must be drawn. This is the paradox that the very theory which seeks to unveil these hidden realities underlying human society also comes into direct collision with them, or rather with the repressing forces which safeguard them in the unconscious of each one of us. If the primary function of repression is to prevent the return of the repressed, it clearly follows that any theory which describes that repressed material runs the risk of being confused with it and coming under attack just as the original repressed elements would do if they attempted to struggle back into consciousness. Against such threats the ego has many defences, such as denial, distortion, forgetting, intellectualization, projection and so on;[15] and thus it comes about that, in the not uncommon tendency to confuse the theory with the fact of what is repressed, psychoanalysis itself is seen as a threat to the very process of repression which it was the first to discover and is itself subjected to these defensive reactions.

The simple consequence is that, being so deeply buried in the human unconscious, any attempt to uncover the repressed foundations of our social life is bound to encoun-

---

[15] For a comprehensive catalogue of these, along with the classic statement of psychoanalytic theory regarding them, see Anna Freud, *The Ego and the Mechanisms of Defence*.

ter severe resistances, especially in the minds of those who have convinced themselves that there is no psychic trauma at the origin of human society and no painful consequences of it hidden within every one of us. But such a bland and anodyne approach will fail even to begin to understand the basis of human society and is certainly not competent to uncover the true causes of our present social unrest. In order to do so we must go back to the very beginning of society, explain the original trauma and then consider what consequences it has had for modern times; for, as we shall see in a later chapter, an inability to accept the truth about ourselves and our societies is probably the most dangerous threat to the successful solution of our present cultural crisis and is certainly the chief obstacle to progress in the sciences of man.

The simple fact is that making the prehistoric — that is, the repressed — part of the mind conscious is a vital aspect of the further development of the ego because conscious insight into itself and its motivation is essential to the ego's rationality and competence in administering and mastering the instinctual drives of the id. For countless generations man could get by without such insight because the automatic, unconscious defensive measures of the primitive ego were effective. Whether such a primitive level of ego-development and insight is appropriate today is a question to which we shall have to return in due course.

The theory of the traumatic beginnings of human culture which I have just summarized seems to explain much about both the ego and society, but it does have one very obvious weakness. The reader will probably object that a hideous primal trauma of parricide and rape is all very well for purposes of explaining the subsequent guilt and neurotic inhibitions of the perpetrators of these ghastly crimes, but can hardly hope to explain how they succeeded in transmitting their new-found superegos to their children, and certainly will not explain how, when all the primal fathers were gone (a process which may have taken a considerable period of time admittedly, but which must have happened eventually), when there were no more primal parricides to be procured, human societies could still construct their civilization on the acquisition of the superego.

This question really resolves itself into a very specific one, which is this: How do individuals of subsequent generations 'inherit' the primal trauma and its consequences? Freud's own answer to this question was that, in part, it may be accounted for by the supposition of an 'archaic heritage' of unconscious memories which go back to primeval times. Whatever the truth of this suggestion, it is nevertheless clear that other, less speculative mechanisms can be suggested. The researches of Theodor Reik[16] and myself[17] have established that in the original hunting societies initiation ritual and religious rites in general fulfilled this function.

The fact that the maintenance of the hunting bands depended on a traumatic event and its consequences meant that those bands had a reason for needing to repeat the trauma, or at least some effective representation of it, and thereby to perpetuate its consequences — the taboos forbidding incest and parricide. This was achieved by a religious ritual which may have stemmed from one in which the original parricides mutilated themselves (and especially the organ which was responsible for their incestuous desires) out of remorse and guilt at what they had done and in mourning for the primal father. Up until very recently men in the most archaic human societies — those in central Australia — ritually mutilated their sexual

---

[16] See the study of initiation ritual in *Ritual*, New York, 1959.
[17] *The Psychoanalysis of Culture*, pp. 16–31.

organs in the course of sacred totemic ceremonies in which, as we have already seen, the primal father is worshipped in the guise of the totem of the brother-clan. This, then, seems to be a repetition of the consequences of the trauma, a ritual of guilt and remorse; but the trauma is re-enacted principally in the initiation of the young men.

As long as boys remain sexually immature they are of no real significance as far as the primal, sexually motivated conflict between sons and fathers is concerned. Consequently, children in aboriginal societies, as the work of Roheim shows, are not subject to any educative or disciplinary measures of any consequence. As children, they pose no threat to the group. But, once the males mature sexually, the primeval antagonism between fathers and sons, egoism and altruism, once again rears its head. At this point the sons are painfully and traumatically initiated — that is, they are subjected to brutal assaults, frightening experiences, are deprived of their mothers and all normal support and, usually at the climax of these experiences, are symbolically castrated by means of some customary mutilation (very often the rather close equivalent represented by circumcision, but otherwise by knocking out of teeth, pulling out of nails, loss of fingers, etc.). Young lads who up to this point have had no real demands made on them by society, who have been spoiled and indulged by their mothers, who have followed their own inclinations entirely and have been tolerated in nearly everything, suddenly and incomprehensibly find that they are the subjects of a spiteful atrocity in which they are abused, assaulted, victimized, mutilated and sometimes threatened with death itself. In societies in which adolescence as we know it does not really occur, they make the transition from childhood to adulthood in one traumatic experience just as their ancestors, generations before, made the change from the innocence of nature to the guilt and responsibility of culture by perpetuating the primal crimes of incest and parricide. In both cases the shock had to be overwhelming and painful in the extreme if it was to generate the civilizing consequences of respect for, and maintenance of, the great taboos of civilization.

The fact that it is only at puberty that initiation occurs today and that it was only at this age that young males came to pose a threat to the peace and stability of early human societies seems to have had, quite apart from its evident social and psychological consequences, important physiological ones as well. There is very considerable evidence which I have reviewed at length elsewhere[18] that, since parting company with the ancestors of today's great apes and since acquiring numerous gelada-like adaptations, the human race has been subject to an evolutionary process known as *neoteny* or *foetalization*. The consequence of this is that human beings have increasingly come to resemble in their adult form the immature — or even foetal — forms of their early ancestors by means of a tendency to delay their individual development and to retain into maturity characteristics which typified the immature stages of their predecessors. Such a trend in evolution cannot be reconciled with gelada-like foraging because its principal outcome was to cause human beings to be born in progressively more helpless and 'retarded' states of development requiring longer and longer maternal care. The career of a full-time vegetarian forager, always on the move in search of food, cannot include patterns of child-care which make such demands on the mother and which put the neonate in such a dependent state. Accordingly, therefore, there is no trace of neotenous tendencies among modern gelada baboons.

However, there is little doubt that this phenomenon is a

[18] *Ibid.*, pp. 39–51.

most important one in our species and it can only be explained by assuming that, with the beginnings of hunting, neotenous changes suddenly became adaptive. The reason why they did so was that in the case of man neoteny was an evolutionary trend largely in the service of ego and superego development. This was because it first and foremost provided for our species' impressive pattern of brain-growth. A large brain relative to body size is an almost universal foetal characteristic of vertebrates, and certainly of mammals. Thus the relatively more immature state of the human neonate, while posing formidable problems for the mother (formidable problems which only communal hunting as a way of life could begin to solve), nevertheless bestowed immense advantages in terms of cerebral development by guaranteeing that human beings were born with progressively larger brains. Further, the retardation of maturity not only preserved a better brain/body-weight ratio but also extended the period of educability and cognitive development which characterizes primate childhoods. Finally, by postponing sexual maturity by the same token, neotenous trends in human evolution ensured that young males stayed as long as possible under the protection of the parental group before being ejected and having to begin to fend for themselves. Such a tendency probably favoured individual survival, particularly in a situation in which hunting — a skill which has to be learned — was coming to be the dominant subsistence activity.

Such considerations were probably crucial before initiation ritual developed to deal with the conflicts between sons and fathers; but even after such conflicts had become institutionalized and ritualized neoteny had an important role to play in postponing the age of initiation by opening up that gap in human psycho-sexual development which Freud called the latency period and which, as we shall see, is an important factor in considering the social and mental health of modern societies.

Whilst there are undoubted cultural factors acting on the latency phenomenon, as Freud himself recognized, he nevertheless maintained that it rested on a biological, innate foundation.[19] Modern research has shown that the innate factors at work seem largely to affect what we might call ego-development. A recent summary of this research states that 'The greater stability and invariance of mental process and the new cognitive structure at seven . . . permit the *inhibition and control of drives* and the postponement of action.'[20] It supports the contention that around the age of seven innate behavioural and neurological changes promote the functioning of the ego in its basic tasks of drive-management, decision-making and postponement of gratification — all features which typify human intelligent and adaptive behaviour over automatic instinctual response. The authors add that by about this age, 'Stable structures have replaced earlier instabilities and can now be used in the service of new cognitive skills while keeping sexual drive components in greater isolation.'[21] Thus it seems that following the early manifestations of the id and its component sexual and agressive drives in early childhood, from about the age of seven until the age of puberty a period of relative quiessence and control of the id sets in, associated with the development of the ego and especially of the superego. During the latency period Freud observed that there was normally an observable de-sexualization of feelings, along with the emergence of such reactions as shame and disgust.

Echoing another observation by Freud, the authors of the recent study note that 'The superego in its function as a

[19] *Three Essays on the Theory of Sexuality*, VII, pp. 177–8; *An Autobiographical Study*, XX, p. 37n.
[20] T. Shapiro and R. Perry, 'Latency revisited', *Psychoanalytic Study of the Child*, XXXI (1976), p. 97 (authors' italics).
[21] *Ibid.*

guiding pilot seems to utilize internalized verbal prohibitions',[22] and point out that the efficacy of verbal regulation seems to be linked to the time-table of brain growth, and in particular to the maturation of the frontal lobes, themselves one of the major cerebral acquisitions produced by the process of neoteny in man: 'The frontal lobe comprises about one third of the hemispheric surface; it includes the primary motor areas, the premotor areas, and frontal eye fields.'[23] Quoting another study they add that the frontal lobe 'represents a relatively late phylogenetic acquisition which is well developed only in primates, especially in Man.'[24] Yet another author they quote 'stresses the importance of frontal lobes in maturation, stating that in children with frontal lesions, behaviour is disinhibited and they are consequently less educable.'[25] The study concludes that 'Such a relationship of the frontal lobes to self-regulation, particularly verbal self-regulation, is of central importance to psychoanalytic concepts of superego and ego controls which are expected following the resolution of the Oedipus complex.'[26]

Summarizing our findings so far we may conclude that the ego, far from emerging fully formed, in fact underwent a very lengthy and indeed complex process of development in the evolution of the human race. Its emergence marked the true beginnings of the specifically human line of behavioural development, and the late acquisition of the superego characterized the beginnings of human culture, religion and civilization in general. We shall now see that

[22] Ibid., p. 100.
[23] ibid., p. 88.
[24] Ibid., quoting R. Truex and M. Carpenter, *Human Neuroanatomy*.
[25] Ibid., quoting W. R. Russell, 'Functions of the frontal lobes', *Lancet* (1948).
[26] Ibid., p. 89.

in order to account for changes in the modern world this evolutionary background of the ego and superego is by no means irrelevant; on the contrary, we must take it very seriously if we are to be able to understand what is going on around us.

2

Beyond the Primal Parricide

Before we come to the consideration of the ego and superego in modern times, we must first accomplish one further task. This is to recapitulate briefly what we might term the cultural, as opposed to the natural, history of the ego and the superego.

Reverting for a moment to the last chapter, we saw that we could answer the question of how it is that subsequent generations could acquire the superego organization produced by the primal trauma of human civilization, but only is so far as our answer was limited to archaic hunting societies like those in central Australia. What of our own, where initiation ritual does not exist? Furthermore, how can an analysis like this, focusing on the most remote past and on the most archaic present-day societies, give us any insight into modern ones afflicted with the problems of scientific and technological progress? To answer these questions we must be prepared to go some little way beyond Freud's *Totem and Taboo* and seek a more general theory. It is to the development of this theory and its application to modern times that the remainder of this book will be devoted.

If we examine the theory of the origins of human society and personality put forward by Freud in *Totem and Taboo* we find that it is what might be termed a *monotraumatic* theory. In other words, it attributes everything to one specific event and draws all its consequences from that one event. Now, as we have already seen, such a monotraumatic theory holds perfectly well for archaic societies, like those in Australia, and explains a great deal about most other primitive cultures (especially those with initiation), and even quite a lot about rather more advanced ones. But for some other socieities its explanatory value is rather more limited. For instance, if we look at religious culture, we can see that the monotraumatic theory is outstandingly good for totemism, the totemic aspects of polytheism and many aspects of monotheism. But for much else in polytheism and monotheism it is of more limited value. Again, it tells us much about the society of archaic hunters and gatherers, but much less about modern or ancient socieities with well-developed, centralized-state structures.

The situation which we find with regard to the *Totem and Taboo* analysis is comparable to that which applies to Einstein's papers on special relativity. Like special relativity, the monotraumatic theory is a restricted one, applicable only to certain specified frames of reference. What it requires to extend it is what Einstein's work on general relativity gave to the special theory, namely, a generalization of it which extends it to all frames of reference regardless. Such an extension will not invalidate the special theory but will fill it out to meet the requirements of wider applicability.

It is in this sense of extension of the basic, restricted theory, that I offer what I would call for the purposes of this discussion, the *polytraumatic* theory. This theory holds that, although human society originated as Freud described it in *Totem and Taboo*, subsequent social evolution led to repetitions and expansion of that primal trauma which, although on a smaller scale than the original one, nevertheless share something of its traumatic nature and crucial consequences — particularly for the subsequent evolution of the superego. We shall find that it is the second and third of these recapitulations and expansions of the primal trauma which are of special relevance to an understanding of modern social conditions and present-day ego-psychology.

As we saw, the primal trauma was associated with a fundamental change in economy, from individualistic vegetarian foraging like that found in modern open-country primates, to communal big-game hunting. Lacking instinctive predispositions to the latter, the change of basic mode of subsistence had to be traumatic, and so it was. It is the contention of the polytraumatic theory that exactly the same thing occurred when the next fundamental change in subsistence-pattern occurred, namely that from hunting and gathering to agriculture. Here, as in the comparable case of the beginnings of hunting, no traumatic consequences have previously been suspected; but it is my view that the transition to cultivation from hunting and gathering was indeed traumatic, both socially and psychologically, and furthermore that the complex details of this secondary trauma, while recapitulating many elements of the first, also anticipated many later ones, including that at the root of our modern malaise.

In fact, one of the first, but also most important aspects of the traumatic change to cultivation can be detected in some advanced hunter-gatherer societies. It is important to make the distinction, when discussing these societies, betwen *delayed* and *immediate-return* subsistence.[1] So far, I have discussed the hunting economy purely as an immediate-return one, and such indeed it is in central

---

[1] We owe this vital distinction to my colleague, Dr James Woodburn: 'Hunters and gatherers today and reconstruction of the past' in E. Gellner (ed.), *Soviet and Western Anthropology*, London, 1980.

Beyond the Primal Parricide

Australia and must have been in the case of the first hunters. The immediate-return system is most likely to be found in localities in which the growing-season is long or year-round and in which ambient temperatures make the storing and preservation of food difficult for peoples at the palaeolithic level of culture. These immediate-return hunter-gatherers never suffer anxiety about the future of food supplies and are characterized by improvident, generous, happy-go-lucky personalities. This is because weaning is either non-existent or very late and because child-rearing is extremely indulgent. Roheim's research in central Australia, for instance, shows that mothers will never refuse a child the breast, even if this means that a younger sibling is displaced by the elder one and suffers malnutrition — possibly to the point of death — as a result. Even quite old children will sometimes be seen at the breast, long after they have begun to eat an adult diet, sucking not so much for sustenance as for emotional consolation.

However, delayed-return systems are quite different in this respect. In hunter-gatherer societies where food is stored, perhaps as in palaeolithic Europe, for the winter, the improvident, take-no-thought-for-the-morrow character of the immediate-return hunter-gatherer has to be modified. Whilst such an attitude to life is clearly desirable for hunters depending on highly unreliable food resources which would soon reduce them to chronic anxiety if they were to take a less prodigal view of things, it is evidently less suitable for seasonal hunters who must store food if they are to avoid starvation. In these societies the beginnings of weaning and disciplined child-rearing can be seen, and it is significant that, associated with the seasonal hunters of the Palaeolithic period in Europe and elsewhere, we find the first female figurines.

In my view, these figurines are evidence of the first consequences of the coming Neolithic trauma — the beginning of weaning and the loss of the primal mothers. We saw that the chief consequence of the change from foraging to hunting was the restitution of the primal father in the totem-animal which was worshipped, and also in the totemic taboos in which his moral authority lived on. Exactly the same occurred with the coming of cultivation and the loss of the primal mother. Now children began to be weaned traumatically at an early age and subject to parental authority in childhood. The effect of this, of course, is to induce an ability to postpone oral instinctual gratification along with a concern about the availability of food — a character ideally suited to the demands of delayed-return systems of subsistence such as seasonal hunter-gatherering or, still more, cultivation. But a direct consequence of this was the appearance of a mother-goddess whose fecund body and ample breasts promised a phantasy-gratification for all that the delayed-return subsistence systems denied.

Sandor Rado, in an article devoted to the elucidation of manic-depressive disorders, expresses the opinion that 'At the bottom of the melancholiac's profound dread of impoverishment there is really simply a dread of starvation ... drinking at the mother's breast remains the radiant image of unremitting, forgiving love,' and he adds that 'It is certainly no mere chance that the Madonna nursing the Child has become the emblem of a mighty religion and thereby the emblem of a whole epoch in our Western civilization.'[2]

I have pointed out elsewhere[3] that the epoch of Western civlization to which Rado refers is dominated by a process of unconscious recapitulation of polytheism in Christian-

---

[2] 'The problem of melancholia', *International Journal of Psychoanalysis*, 9 (1928), p. 427.
[3] *The Psychoanalysis of Culture*, ch. 4, sec. I.

Beyond the Primal Parricide

ity. The Madonna and Child probably do carry the symbolic meaning which he attributes to them; but if this is so then it is one which much earlier was carried by the representations of Isis nursing Horus, or by the many-breasted Diana of Ephesus, herself a lineal descendant of Palaeolithic figurines like the Venus of Willendorf. The heavy breasts and opulent maternal figures of the old Stone Age goddesses which give way to the multiplied breasts of the Ephesian Diana and then to the Mother-and-Child images mentioned above represent a trend of increasing clarification and refinement of the basic psychological situation — the need to find in heaven a substitute for the primal mother lost on earth. It emphasizes that what is important is not the fecund earth-mother herself so much as the dependent relation of the child to her and to her nutritive, sustaining functions. The immaculately conceived Mother of God with the Christ Child is apparently only one of the latest — although, as we shall see later, not *the* latest — and most idealized versions of this idea.

As long ago as 1938, Edith Weigert-Vowinkel, in a surprisingly little-known, but remarkable article, recognized that what she terms 'early planter culture' was characterized by mother-goddess worship and by manic-depressive tendencies. She observed, following Abraham that

> the fixation of the boy on his mother in the transition period from the oral to the anal phase, that is, in the transition from the purely receptive interests of the child to his first productive efforts, may have a fatal outcome; it may leave behind a disposition to manic-depressive affections. Matriarchal planter culture appears not to have overcome this difficulty of development completely. Masculine development did not detach itself from the nourishing mother. The ideal of the fecund mother goddess, the cults

of fecundity indicate constant anxiety as to fertility, similar to the fear of starvation in depressive patients.[4]

The appearance of a weaning-trauma in early agricultural cultures explains the paradox of why it is that a loss of the ideal mother — that is, a frustration — leads to an over-involvement with her. The oral-maternal fixation which Weigert-Vowinkel mentions in this quotation is the outcome of a frustration; the fixation being, fundamentally, a rebellion against the inflicted loss of the breast and an attachment to its memory. At the same time, my own researches into the origins of agriculture suggest that the women who were responsible for the discovery and early development of cultivation were motivated by drives of a masculine, aggressive kind and were unlikely to tolerate lengthy breast-feeding and the demands of selfless child-care[5] but also, like their modern equivalents, tended to develop strong narcissistic identifications with their male children (the masculine woman's substitute penis). Such mothers may have created an oral-maternal fixation in their children by their early and traumatic weaning of them, but would also have maintained them in a passive and otherwise dependent state, not because of their passive maternal solicitude, but because of their aggressive, assertive masculinity which caused them to dominate their children rather as a father might.

In his paper on 'Mourning and Melancholia' Freud established that in depression following the loss of a love-object the ego absorbs that object into itself so that the exaggerated self-reproaches, self-deprecation and self-hatred which typify the condition can be understood as sadistic drives which have been unconsciously directed on

---

[4] 'The cult and mythology of the Magna Mater from the standpoint of psychoanalysis', *Psychiatry*, I (1938), p. 364.
[5] *The Psychoanalysis of Culture*, pp. 85–93.

to the object whose 'shadow has fallen on the ego.'[6] This identification with, and punishment of, the mother-goddess is vividly portrayed in what Edith Weigert-Vowinkel says about the cult of the Phrygian goddess Cybele and her castrated son, Attis. The priests of Cybele

> identified themselves with the dying god, in order to dedicate themselves to the goddess. They worked themselves into a state of frenzy near unconsciousness by means of dizzy swirling dances with excessive contortions of the body, accompanied by the violent stimulation of the rhythm of monotonous music .... They inflicted wounds on themselves in the sword dance and castigated themselves with ankle whips made of leather and bone, sprinkling the altar of the goddess with their blood. This continued until at the peak of exaltation on ... March 24, every one ... voluntarily castrated himself, cutting off the entire genitals with a consecrated stone knife .... Women who consecrated themselves to the goddess in like manner cut off one or both breasts.[7]

Thereafter the male priests dressed as women: 'To be filled with the Great Mother, to be possessed by her, was the only form of life they desried.'[8]

If I am right about the masculine character of the women pioneers of agriculture we can see that the fact that the followers of the Phrygian mother-goddess castrated themselves is a nice illustration of Freud's idea of the 'shadow of the object falling on the ego': the ultimate reproach against the new agricultural mother was that she was masculine, and therefore the self-punishment came to fit her crime while confirming the identification with her in the most exact way possible.

Yet such extreme examples of self-multilation, although

---

[6] XIV, p. 249.
[7] 'The cult and mythology of the Magna Mater'
[8] Ibid., p. 353.

by no means unknown elsewhere among worshippers of the mother-goddess, are, as might be expected, far from universal. Much more common, and much more readily recognizable as collective expressions of depressive tendencies, are the ceremonial 'wailings of Tammuz' celebrated in ancient Mesopotamia, or the mourning for the dead Osiris which figured so prominently in his cult in ancient Egypt. Ritual mourning for the divine son of a mother-goddess is very common throughout ancient polytheism — not to mention modern polytheisms like Catholicism — where it seems to represent the same situation as the self-inflicted mutilations but at one remove. Now the followers of the cult identify with a son-god like Adonis, Attis or Osiris — not to mention Christ — who in himself comprises both the fixated worshipper of the mother (Madonna and Child) and the punished mother herself (*pietà*). Instead of completely introjecting the mother and emasculating himself in his unconscious desire to be revenged on her, the believer can make do with an identification with a mythical son who has done just this (the crucified Christ). Finally, it is worth mentioning the possibility that the traditional sadness and dejection with which the first crops were cut in Egypt,[9] or the seed was sown in Greece and elsewhere[10] originates in the same unconscious depressive complex. Here, depressive feelings associated with the originators of agriculture — the weaning mothers of the first, and every, cultivating generation — seem to have become displaced on to the new subsistence-pattern itself. Certainly, it is remarkable that Greek drama, which is known to have evolved out of ancient religious rites, clearly polarized into two opposite tendencies: the depressive in the tragedy, and the manic in

[9] J. Frazer, *Adonis, Attis, Osiris (Part IV, The Golden Bough*, London, 1936), II, p. 45.
[10] J. Frazer, *Spirits of the Corn and Wild (*Part V. *The Golden Bough)*, I, p. 46.

the comedy. It is to the latter pole of the conflict that we must now turn.

The psychological developments which have just been discussed were the consequences of a traumatic loss, that of the primal mother, and were responses to it. But not all the responses were depressive. We know from the study of modern depressive individuals that their illness, if it is of the type termed manic-depressive, can take a sometimes sudden and completely opposite course. Instead of being melancholic, withdrawn and dejected, the individual, for no apparent reason, begins to show the opposite symptoms and becomes instead exuberantly outward-going, supremely confident and widly excited. In some especially interesting and puzzling cases these manic interludes alternate regularly with the depressive ones, sometimes with so-called 'periods of remission' in between.

This phenomenon in individual psychopathology has an exact and illuminating parallel in early agricultural societies which has until recently gone unnoticed. In *The Psychoanalysis of Culture* I drew attention to the megalomania of early divine kingships without, at the time, seeing its relation to the depressive aspects of the early agriculture on which these institutions were based.[11] Nevertheless, it is now clear, as I hope to show, that the two opposite types of symptom do in fact appear in connection with the coming of agriculture and, which is more to the point for our present concerns, that this is a phenomenon not without relevance to the understanding of the modern world.

In his discussion of the problem in 'Mourning and Melancholia' Freud offers the initial hypothesis that mania is to be understood as a state in which the ego appears to have got over its loss of the object with the consequence

[11] pp. 65–7, 132, 151.

that the instinctual drives previously fixated on it are now liberated — giving rise to the boundless energy and enthusiasm of the manic condition.[12] A parallel phenomenon seems to occur in early agricultural societies when mounting economic surpluses make possible the emergence of chiefs, kings and even emperors. In *The Psychoanalysis of Culture* I drew attention, following a hint by Freud, to the fact that the new agricultural potentates were obvious re-embodiments of the primal father and of his tyrannous, sedentary and hierarchic domination. But, in so far as they are to be seen as sons of the lost primal mother, they clearly represent the manic alternative to the depressive self-punishment of the followers of Cybele or the castrated and killed sons of the Great Mother represented by Attis and Tammuz, by the dead and dismembered Osiris, or the crucified Christ. (Indeed, the latter in his resurrection seems to point directly to this alternative, and we should not forget that such a comparatively late example as this had a clear and much earlier precedent in the resurrection of Osiris.)

Nevertheless, it may well be that the best symbolic account of the more specifically manic response to the loss of the all-providing pre-agricultural mother is to be found in the oldest epic poem known to us — the ancient Babylonian *Epic of Gilgamesh*. At the beginning of the poem Gilgamesh is portrayed, like the Pharaohs of the ancient Egyptian *Pyramid Texts*,[13] very much as the returned primal father: 'his arrogance has no bounds by day or night. No son is left with his father . . . His lust leaves no virgin to her lover, neither the warrior's daughter or the wife of the noble.'[14] Yet Gilgamesh is not contented. Although is is king of Uruk, possessor of perfect

---

[12] XIV, p. 255.
[13] Badcock, *The Psychoanalysis of Culture* pp. 64-7.
[14] *The Epic of Gilgamesh* (ed. N. K. Sandars), Harmondsworth, 1980, p. 62.

beauty, laden with gifts by the gods and two-thirds divine, he still feels a need to set up his name 'in the place where the names of famous men are written . . . I am committed to this enterprise: To climb the mountain, to cut down the cedar, and leave behind me an enduring name.'[15]

Such heroic ambition reminds one of the ambition which can frequently be seen in sons of mothers who have made their children too dependent on them but who are themselves ambitious and agressive and unconsciously see their male children as their own frustrated masculinity — in the concrete terms in which the unconscious always thinks, as their penis. Such sons can either succumb to being the passsive agent of their mothers' neurotic ambitions or can try to rebel, often in a manner which seeks to be both a proof of the son's independent masculinity and a revolt against the awesome maternal authority. Such men frequently become misogynistic, aggressive towards all women (whom they unconsciously perceive as phallic and dominating) and reveal evidence of homosexual tendencies.

The latter are clearly evidenced by Gilgamesh, who contemptuously repudiates the normally irresistible advances of Ishtar, goddess of love, but whose feelings for his friend Enkidu are 'like those of a man for a woman'.[16]

A revolt against the phallic mother may also explain the puzzling imagery of the cedar forest which Gilgamesh cuts down with such disastrous effect. As Neumann[17] and other writers have pointed out, trees are probably understood by the unconscious to be the phallus of Mother Earth. Certainly, it is interesting that trees in general, and, more especially, the more phallic-shaped cypresses and other evergreens, play a significant role in the myths associated with the Attis cult (not to mention the cases of

[15] *Ibid.*, pp. 70–73.
[16] *Ibid.*, p. 66.
[17] E. Neumann, *The Great Mother*, London, 1955, p. 49.

Adonis, Tammuz,[18] Osiris — and, if we are correct in seeing the Cross as a tree — Christ). In one of these,[19] Agdistis, a hermaphrodite, born of the seed of Zeus and Mother Earth, is castrated by having the male genitals torn off *through being tied to a tree* — a not exactly common method, the reader will agree. The blood from this lost organ then causes another tree to spring up! If the son is psychologically castrated by a too-close tie to the phallic mother, then the symbolism of this myth is very transparent. (Later in the same version of the myth Attis castrates himself under a pine tree. In other versions of the myth a spruce tree grows on the spot where Attis buries his genitals; and in the Attis and Cybele cult in particular, and in agricultural ritual in general, trees, May-poles, wooden pillars and crosses play a very important part.)

Such considerations as these suggest that the feat of Gilgamesh in cutting down the cedar forest, besides its undoubted socio-economic significance (wood was scarce in Uruk, and kings had to be great builders), was really one of successful symbolic castration of the phallic mother — in other words, the son's successful defence of his own masculinity. This is what Gilgamesh has to prove: over and above this obvious status as Father, he has to show that he has overcome his attachment to the phallic Mother.

In Greek mythology, as one might expect, many examples of heroes who resemble Gilgamesh can be found, and it is likely that the Amazons are to be understood as mythological recollections of the traumatic character of the impact of the new, aggressive and masculine child-rearing regimes of the mothers of early agriculture. In a psychoanalytic study of the Amazons Bernice Schultz

---

[18] G. Widengren, *The King and the Tree of Life in Ancient Near Eastern Religion*, Uppsala, 1951-4, p. 15.
[19] Weigert-Vowinkel, 'The cult and Mythology of the Magna Mater, p. 356; B. S. Engle, 'Attis, A Study in Castration', *Psychoanalytic Review*, 23 (1936), pp. 363ff.

Beyond the Primal Parricide

Engle points out that according to tradition they 'cared nothing for womanly arts, spent ten months of the year farming, pasturing cattle, and especially in training horses. The strongest spent much of their time practicing military exercises and hunting on horseback.'[20] The term 'Amazon' was explained either as being a derivation from a word meaning 'without a breast', or from the meaning 'unsuckled'.[21] Either way, the word seems to suggest that it was their inability or refusal to suckle which was regarded as characteristic — a supposition exactly in line with my theory that they represent the masculine, aggressive, weaning mothers of early agriculture. This makes intelligible the observation that 'in no work of art extant is an Amazon portrayed with infant or child', and that in Greek literature the most common epithets associated with the Amazons were terms like 'man-hating', 'warlustful', 'dauntless', 'fearless', 'man-subduing'.[22] Finally, it is worth noting Engle's remark that the horse on which the Amazon warrior rode into battle represented 'a substitute for the phallic power which she envied' and 'made her feel like a man'.[23]

If we now turn our attention to the hero-literature of ancient Greece, it is notable that just about every prominent hero does battle at one time or another, and sometimes repeatedly, with Amazon women. Bellerophon 'slew the Amazons, women peers of men'[24] and Heracles, the most popular of Greek heroes, found that the Ninth Labour assigned to him was to seize the girdle of the Amazon queen. Much of his career in fact seems to have been devoted to Amazon-slaying, but it is significant that

---

[20] 'The Amazons in Ancient Greece', *Psychoanalytic Quarterly*, XI (1942), p. 514.
[21] *Ibid.*, p. 515.
[22] *Ibid.*, p. 517, 518.
[23] *Ibid.*, p. 545.
[24] Homer, *Iliad*, vi, 168-95.

if heroes like Heracles represent the revolt of the son against the phallic mother then they also give evidence of their dependency on her when we find our hero forced to don women's garb and do women's work as proof of his love for the Lydian queen Omphale, while she wears his lion's skin, brandishes his club and spanks him with her slipper if his handiwork does not please her. We could hardly wish for a more graphic portrayal of the son who is tied to his domineering, aggressive mother by ties of love, but who has to be a hero in the eyes of the world to prove his masculine worth. Some accounts of Heracles' exploits stress his misogyny, applying the epithet *misogynos* to him; and it is notable that women were excluded from his shrines. Significantly, on one occasion he was supposed to have wounded Hera *in the breast*.

Comparable remarks could be made about Theseus and Achilles because they too at times wore women's clothes and had their ideal relationship not with a woman, but with a man, as Gilgamesh did. Engle concludes that 'All the heroes rebelled against female domination . . . . All inflicted horrible slaughter on Amazonian women . . . . None achieved a secure heterosexual union.'[25] Their careers seem to have been mythological expressions of the need to overcome the matriarchs who founded agriculture and to whom, in time, the heroes and demi-gods were to be heirs.

If we consider for a moment the extent to which the hero-kings of early agricultural societies did indeed come to play a maternal, provident role with regard to those dependent on them we can perhaps begin to see the truth of the claim that they became the heirs of the matriarchs. In a way which strikingly presages the modern socialist welfare-state, divine kings became not only tyrants, but also providers and protectors of their people. This is

---

[25] 'The Amazons in Ancient Greece', p. 544.

perhaps nowhere more clearly seen than in Inca Peru where the Inca monarch headed an authoritarian welfare state in which his monopoly of the economic surplus, along with his military and policy power, meant that the citizen looked only to him for protection from his fellow men and from hunger, want and hardship. In the ancient Near East similar conditions obtained and in a parallel manner divine despots became leaders of authoritarian welfare states. If the all-provident mother of the hunter-gatherer societies had been lost with the coming of agriculture and weaning so that a divine substitute had had to be found in heaven in the shape of the mother-goddess, then eventually a real, human substitute had been found on earth in the person of the all-powerful emperor or king whose granaries could supply in reality what the opulent breasts of the divine mother promised in phantasy — namely, reassurance against oral anxiety and the fear of hunger.[26] Along with his paternal role as protector of the weak, defender of the state and dispenser of justice, the Inca, Pharaoh or divine king summed up in his person much of the image of the parents in the mind of the child and in the unconscious of the adult. In terms of man's cultural development he represents a royal epiphany of the primal father, an authentic reincarnation of primal despotism.

The fusion of the actual person of a son of the agricultural mother with the divine, pre-agricultural, primal mother-image corresponds to a further, structural description of mania by Freud: namely, one in which the ego and superego have fused together — in genetic terms, in which the parent and child are one.[27] According to Rado, its specific origin is to be found in the blissful unity of mother

---

[26] I follow the psychoanalytic convention of using *phantasy* for the content of unconscious processes and *fantasy* for conscious constructions.

[27] *Group Psychology and the Analysis of the Ego*, XVIII, p. 132.

and child at the breast.[28] If this is so, then we can see how adequately the divine king sums up in his person this state of psychic unity. He is the son of the phallic mother who has overcome her and fused with her to become a living equivalent of the perfect primal mother, not through self-castration (the depressive alternative), but through manic self-assertion: a sentiment nicely summed up in the ritual of Cybele and her son Attis: 'a feeding on milk, as though we were born again; after which rejoicing and garlands and as it were a return to the gods.[29] Rado concludes,

> It is a striking fact that in mania the adult with his manifold potentialities of action and reaction reproduces the uninhibited instinctual manifestations which we observe in the euphoria of the satiated suckling. That the quality of the reactions of a period of life in which the superego did not as yet exist should be the pattern upon which is modelled the manic state (the basis of which is temporary withdrawal of the superego) is exactly what we should expect.[30]

It is equally if not more stricking that these remarks about mania in the individual manic-depressive of modern times hold perfectly true for the cultural equivalent: the first cultivating societies. As we saw earlier, the period in the history of the human race when 'the superego did not exist' was that preceding the primal trauma and coinciding with the foraging way of life of our hominid ancestors. As I have elaborated elsewhere,[31] the early agricultural divine monarchies seem to recapitulate, albeit in purely cultural forms, the natural conditions of that primeval existence: for instance, an economy based on grains (domesticated

[28] 'The Problem of Melancholia', p. 428.
[29] B. Shultz Engle, 'Attis: a study of castration', *Psychoanalytic Review*, (1936), p. 367.
[30] 'The Problem of Melancholia', p. 436.
[31] *The Psychoanalysis of Culture*, pp. 64 ff.

rather than wild), a social structure centred around one dominant, tyrannous male and his harem (now a human state rather than a primate group), and — at least in the case of some ancient Egyptian dynasties — even the recruitment of apprentice heirs-apparent (the institution known as *coregency*). If the modern manic individual is uninhibited in the state of mania because, as Rado suggests, he has regressed to a state of psychic organization that existed in him at his mother's breast and definitely before his superego formed, then we can see that the reason why the divine kings of early agricultural societies could be described as 'manic' lie in exactly similar conditions: a situation in which the ego is not constrained by the superego because their collective equivalents — primal father and mother on the one side, and the son on the the other — have become on in the person of the monarch (who, in this respect, is decidedly and accurately described as an incarnation of the *trinity*).

So much for the son's manic triumph over the phallic mother symbolized by the arrogant domination and tree-felling exploits of Gilgamesh or the Amazon-slaying of the Greek heroes; but what of the homosexual element in the situation to which I alluded earlier? Here we find another remarkable parallel with the psychopathology of modern individuals. According to the findings of psycho-analysis, a conflict surrounding unconscious homosexual elements is at the centre of the psychosis known as paranoia (or paranoid schizophrenia). Clear evidence of comparable phenomena can also be found in some cultures. In *The Psychoanalysis of Culture* I drew attention to the undoubted paranoia of the fanatical adherent of solar monotheism in ancient Egypt, the Pharaoh Akhenaten (alias Amenhotep IV), but at that time I was unable to demonstrate how such paranoid tendencies were related to the evolution of cultivating societies. Now, with the aid of the polytraumatic theory of human social and psychological evolution, such a connection is easy to show.

The essence of the unconscious conflict in paranoia relates more to the parent of the same sex than it does to that of the opposite one. We have already seen that depressive or manic responses may be shown to be related to the problem of the son's relation to the mother and his contradictory desire to be devoted to her as the ideal mother of hunter-gatherer prehistory and yet to be free of her as the phallic, dominant mother of primal agriculture. As we saw, the latter relation threatened to compromise the son's masculinity and to force him into a passive, feminine relation to his mother which could result either in abject surrender, as in depression, or in defiant revolt, as in mania. In paranoid disorders however, it is the son's passive relation to the father that threatens to unman him, and this expresses itself in the characteristic symptom of paranoia — delusions produced by the mechanism of projection.

Projection is a psychological process whereby something which is inside the mind is perceived as being outside it, perhaps in someone else's mind, or in the outside world. Basically it consists in a failure in the ego by means of which inner, subjective sensations become confused with those originating in the outside world — an observation which reveals how close projection is to thoroughgoing hallucination (with which it is, of course, frequently allied in paranoia). Delusion-formation in paranoid disorders makes use of this process to provide defence against the passive homosexual wish. One of the most characteristic forms which this takes is the delusion of megalomania — a state in which the subject believes himself to possess supreme value and ultimate powers:

> I feel so close to God, so inspired by His Spirit that in a

Beyond the Primal Parricide

sense I am God. I see the future, plan the Universe, save mankind; I am utterly and completely immortal; I am even male and female. The whole Universe animate and inanimate, past, present and future is within me. All nature and life, all spirits, are cooperating and connected with me; all things are possible. I am in a sense identical with all spirits from God to Satan. I reconcile Good and Evil and create light, darkness, worlds, universes.[32]

Such a state is clearly closely allied to the mania of the manic-depressive (indeed, this quotation is from an autobiographical account by someone who was predominantly manic-depressive), and our researches into the cultural background of these modern psychopathological conditions allow us to see why this is so. It is because, if mania represents an overcoming of the lost primal mother by means of triumphant substitution of the son for the mother, then megalomania represents, not only a denial of the passive love of the father (*I do not love him, I love myself*[33]), but also an unconscious identification and fusion with him (it is in this sense that our manic autobiography above can claim that 'in a sense I am God', etc.). In both manias fusion with the psychic representative of the parental figure — the superego — occurs with comparable consequences. In both cases the ego seeks to defend itself against a passive relation to the superego and, in its manic symptoms, succeeds in convincing itself that it has been successful.

Yet, of course, even though the conflict in megalomania and other paranoid delusions centres on the father, the cause of the condition, at least in the cultural case which we are examining here, and doubtless in many clinical cases as well, lies in the relationship with the mother.

---

[32] J. Custance, *Wisdom, Madness and Folly*, London, 1951, p. 51.
[33] Freud, 'Psychoanalytic notes upon an autobiographical account of a case of paranoia', XII, p. 65.

Heroes like Gilgamesh or Heracles have unconscious homosexual inclinations because they are misogynistic — that is, because the female love-object is precluded by the conflict with her and because the homosexual equivalent is at least in part pre-determined by the fact that the mother-figure is perceived as essentially *phallic*. The consequence of this is that women are feared because they are seen to be sexually aggressive, and relations with men are spoiled because a close tie to them, which might otherwise constitute a conflict-free alternative nevertheless connotes a parallel threat of passive dependency. Thus conflict is inevitable in either case.

In the Amarna Letters, a library of correspondence dating from XVIIIth dynasty Egypt, Pharaoh is routinely addressed as 'King, Lord, Sungod of the lands, the Sungod from heaven!,[34] and throughout ancient and modern polytheism we encounter worship of the sun and identification of divine kings as sons of the sun. Modern psychotics also often make something of a personal divinity of the sun, as the following quotation suggests:

> The sun came to have an extraordinary effect on me. It seemed to be charged with all power; not merely to symbolize God but actually to be God. Phrases like 'Light of the World', 'the Sun of Righteousness that setteth nevermore' and so on ran through my head without ceasing, and the mere sight of the sun was sufficient greatly to intensify this manic excitement under which I was labouring. I was impelled to address the sun as a personal God, and to evolve little rituals of sunworship.[35]

The psychoanalysis of paranoid delusions regarding the sun leaves little doubt that it usually represents the father.

---

[34] J. B. Pritchard (ed.), *Ancient Near Eastern Texts Relating to the Old Testament*, Princeton, 1969, pp. 483–90.
[35] Custance, *Wisdom, Madness and Folly*, p. 18.

As such, it is normally a benevolent deity; and, indeed, is perceived as such in much of the myth and literature of the solar cults. The image of the sun is obviously suitable for this use because it is the brightest object in the sky, is the source of all life — a scientific fact which was appreciated even in ancient Egypt — and exists in the unapproachable splendour of the empyrean. Perhaps surprisingly then, other, less benevolent themes are also found associated with the solar cult, mainly in the form of the collective delusions of persecution which express themselves as belief in witchcraft.

In his *Golden Bough* Sir James Frazer had difficulty in making up his mind between the two rival theories of the fire-cults and fire-festivals which are found intimately connected with the agricultural year throughout those parts of the world where the sun is neither so bright nor so constant as in the cloudless skies of Egypt. On the one hand, much empirical evidence seems to point to the fact that fire-cults in which fire-wheels are rolled down hills, thrown into the air, or in which bonfires are kindled on Midwinter's or Midsummer's Day all reflect solar symbolism; the object of these practices being to ensure the return of the sun, or protection against its heat or whatever. Yet, on the other hand, an equally impressive body of evidence seems to point to these rites being concerned with witchcraft and its repulsion.[36] But the psychoanalytic theory of paranoia enables us to see that these two equally-well-attested interpretations are not in any way in conflict with one another because in the latent content of paranoia we find both a tendency to symbolize the father as the sun *and* a delusion of persecution concerning him which in a typically paranoid way denies the homosexual factor by saying *I do not love him, he hates me*.[37] The association of paranoid

[36] J. Frazer, *Balder the Beautiful* (Part VII, *The Golden Bough*), I and II.
[37] Freud, 'Psychoanalytic notes upon an autobiographical account of a case of paranoia', XII, p. 63.

delusions of persecution by witches with solar fire-cults is therefore not in the least surprising; in fact, it is exactly what we should have expected.

It is now clear that once more or less traumatic weaning was introduced by mothers who were, by comparison to the hunter-gatherers who preceded them, forceful and disciplinarian, the right psychological conditions existed for the emergence of manic-depressive and paranoid disorders. These could supervene powerfully in the individual personality — as they evidently did in that of Akhenaten — but, more frequently perhaps, these psychopathological tendencies could manifest themselves in the culture of the agricultural society, perhaps as fire-festivals (with attendant witch-delusions) or as full-blown cults of solar-imperial megalomania. (This should not be taken to mean that such psychopathological trends could not appear in individuals before the coming of cultivation or delayed-return hunter-gathering, merely that they would have been much less common and could not have taken on the collective, cultural significance which they did in the Neolithic and subsequent epochs.)

Of course, these pathological tendencies are still with us today and are widely recognized in individual mental illness; but what is not generally appreciated is their extent in cultural forms, not all of which are limited to ancient societies. However, before we pass to a consideration of modern conditions, we must turn our attention to one last aspect of the situation in the Neolithic which, as we shall see, has an important parallel in our own times.

If we pause for a moment and consider the place of the Neolithic revolution in the theory of human personality and society so far advanced in these pages we will be struck by the fact that the coming of cultivation posed a major threat to the psychological foundations of human society as they had evolved up to that point. As we saw in the last chapter, the demands of the hunting economy imposed the need for considerable altruism, cooperation and inhibition of aggression within the hunting band — in other words, the need for the superego. The shifting, nomadic way of life of the primeval hunter-gatherers, along with their inability to store food and their elementary level of technological development meant that rough egalitarianism and fluid relations of superordination and subordination characterized their way of life. Not so the cultivators. Their sedentary way of life, the fact that individual families could become units of production and could not only store considerable surpluses, but pass them on to subsequent generations, now meant that the old egalitarian and cooperative values fo the hunter-gatherers were gone for ever. Now the experience of weaning introduced envy, competitiveness and resentment on a level never seen before. As we have seen, the result was the emergence of social groupings resembling more the rigid hierarchy of the primal horde than the fluid community of the hunting band. Thus individualism, egoism and a brute struggle for social superiority emerged once again, leading ultimately to the supreme tyranny of the god-kings. Such rulers could defend the social order by force assuredly; but by replacing the moral authority of the totem-father with the force of arms and the ingenuities of police control they ran the risk of invalidating the purely psychological and religious prohibitions which had supported the old order and had so successfully promoted human social advancement. Indeed, in their frequently incestuous marriages, and in their usually selfish domination they seriously compromised the fundamental prohibitions against incest and parricide on which all human societies depend.

Perhaps some, or even many, Neolithic societies perished because of this. The persistently repeated rapid rise and fall of civilizations in Central and South America may, for all we know, reflect just this process. But of these failures in the experiment of agricultural society we know next to nothing. Those that survived — particularly those that both survived and thrived, as in ancient Egypt — have left us ample evidence both of the danger, and of how it was met.

Expressed in terms of individual psychology, the danger was one of dissolution of the painfully acquired superego and corresponding regression in the ego. If, as I have tried to show, the acquisition of the ego and superego were such important aspects of economic adaptation, first to hunting and then to cultivation, it is clear that the very success of the latter threatened to compromise the psychological foundations on which it was based. In the main, the danger consisted in a tendency for the external constraints imposed by the tyranny of the agricultural monarchs to come to replace the purely internal, psychological restraint of the superego. In practical terms this meant replacing processes of superego-formation in child-rearing and initiation ritual with mechanisms of state law-enforcement — parallel processes of superego-degradation and increasing state control which, as we shall see, seem well advanced in the modern world and which therefore constitute a similar danger.

Nevertheless, in early agricultural societies that had not developed into totalitarian welfare states child-rearing assumed a new and crucial importance which it had not possessed in the primeval hunter-gatherer societies (except perhaps by default: that is, by not really existing as a means of cultural repression). Now weaning, toilet-training and the instilling of a capacity for self-discipline and instinctual renunciation became crucial for economic survival. A responsible, hard-working and disciplined work-force was required for the exacting demands of agriculture; and these were character traits of such importance and of such a basic nature that their instilling could not be left entirely until puberty and initiation. On the contrary, they began soon after birth and gave to mothers in particular and to child-rearing in general an importance and profundity that was fully reflected in the latent content of the myth and ritual of primitive agricultural peoples but was not in the least consciously understood until the coming of psychoanalysis in the twentieth century.

3

Discontent and its Civilization

Civilization, like the city of Venice, seems to have been built on unprepossessing ground. Like the malarial swamps out of which the Most Serene Republic rose, we have seen that human altruism, communal feeling and social responsibility arose out of the egoistic, sadistic and erotic drives with which nature had endowed man. Yet, again like Venice, this far-from-ideal situation turned out to have hidden advantages of its own. Just as the first Venetians found that the water-logged islands of their lagoon, far from merely affording them protection from their enemies on land, also provided them with ideal access to the sea and with it immense possibilities of wealth and naval power, so it emerged in the course of human social evolution that the psychological mechanisms which had been necessary in socializing man also proved serviceable for many other enterprises and in time produced the great flowering of human culture which we see around us today. Yet — and here again the comparison with Venice seems particularly appropriate — there is evidence that in recent times those foundations of society have begun to crumble and decay so that, just like the *Serenissima*, society today faces ever higher spring tides of modernity which threaten to overwhelm the traditional basis of the social order, perhaps even to destroy it altogether.

The point was made earlier that psychoanalysis could sometimes be confused with a process of liberation of basic drives and anti-social tendencies. Of course, this view is based on a foolish misapprehension; but it is probably nevertheless true that a mistaken view of psychoanalysis, and a misuse of its teachings, has contributed in no small part to our present social predicament. In the early days of psychoanalysis Freud's findings regarding the existence of infantile sexuality were hotly and indignantly denied. Yet, of course, infantile sexuality is a reality, as no honest observer of children can deny. Since the denial of reality is always a troublesome defence against unwelcome truths, a characteristic shift has occurred whereby the reality of the phenomenon is no longer denied as such but its significance is discounted. The result is that 'in place of the denial of infantile sexuality we have the "permissiveness" which, as it were, does not take the drives seriously.'[1]

So says a recent study which deals with the modern trend in child-rearing and its consequences for both the individual and society. Its authors point to the relative rarity of hysteria nowadays when compared with its frequent occurrence before the First World War:

> 'As hysteria results from the repression of sexuality in the child's upbringing, the marked change in society's attitudes towards sex has made the conspicuous symptoms disappear. This can be confirmed by the occasional occurrence of the former symptoms of hysteria in areas where family upbringing has not changed. Where the environment has changed, the symptoms of hysteria have been replaced by a multitude of character neuroses and psychosomatic manifestations. Optimistic views, not shared by Freud, that liberation from sexual prohibitions would eli-

---

[1] H. and Y. Lowenfeld, 'Our permissive society and the superego', *Psychoanalytic Quarterly*, 39 (1970), p. 592. The authors have kindly given their permission for the extensive quotation here.

minate neurosis and make for a healthier society have proved to be wrong.[2]

They add that

> Although Freud saw 'civilized society perpetually threatened with disintegration', apparently he did not foresee how far society would go in the liberation of instinctual drives.... Freud may not have forseen that it would be a difficult task for parents to consciously recognize infantile sexuality without being seduced into the role of a participant. The incest taboo lost its firm ground with the lifting of the parents' repression and is now only half-heartedly observed.[3]

They point out that discontent with civilization, rather than diminishing because of the new 'liberated' and permissive attitude, has instead increased. If, as was argued earlier, drive-inhibition in the service of civilization is effectively a matter of accepting and internalizing the prohibitions of the father — in other words, of developing a superego — then their next point is entirely to be expected:

> Drive liberation, the consequence of the exercise by the older generation of less pressure on the younger generation, has not diminished the conflict between generations, but heightened it. Sexual liberation and the easier opportunity of sexual gratification for today's youth have not produced a lessening of aggression.[4]

How could it? It is clear that if the theory advanced in these pages is correct then lessening of parental authority can only lead to increasing confrontation with the younger generation. If the maintenance of the essential taboos

[2] *Ibid.*, p. 591.
[3] *Ibid.*, pp. 593–4.
[4] *Ibid.*, p. 594.

against incest and agression against the father are the foundation of the superego and of human society everywhere, it follows as a matter of simple inevitability that liberation of sexual drives which are fundamentally incestuous in their infantile and unconscious origins should lead to conflict with the fathers. As we saw earlier, it was out of this primal conflict that human societies and the superego first emerged. Should these primeval conflicts re-appear without effective means of resolution or containment, then we are justified in saying that the foundations of modern society, like the rotting wooden piles on which the city of Venice stands, are in danger of erosion, perhaps even of total dissolution:

> All moral rules it seems, derive their strength from the original incest taboo and lose their reliability if this taboo is weakened. But the consequences of an unresolved oedipus complex look quite different today from the way they looked in Freud's time. The question is how the sexual liberation in family and society has altered the development of the superego. 'Permissiveness' has reduced the father's role as the strong and forbidding one . . . .
>
> There has always been a wide discrepancy in the superego between the infantile image of the parents and the later one in which the characteristics of the real parents predominate. The changes in our civilization have considerably enlarged this discrepancy. The image of the real parents contrasts more and more with the early infantile one, and this contrast includes others who become part of the superego, teachers and other authority figures . . . today we have the following problem: the inhibiting, controlling, and guiding function of the superego, which largely merges with the ego, is weakened through the weakness of the parents, through indulgent education which fails to train the ego, and through the general social climate of permissiveness. The sexual and aggressive drives are much less under the guidance of rules. But the

severe superego of early childhood still lives in the individual. The result is restlessness, discontent, depressive moods, craving for substitute satisfactions.[5]

The authors of this study point out that because today's youth is being failed by the parental generation where the all-important factor of mature superego-formation is concerned youth has turned to the more primitive and regressive superego-formation found in groups. As Freud demonstrated in *Group Psychology and the Analysis of the Ego*, typical group psychology produces a lowering of the ego-competence of the individual group member in favour of the group itself and especially of the leader who takes over important ego-functions from him, principally those appertaining to the superego. This is why individuals in groups can show marked degradation in their intellectual and critical powers and why they can be induced to do things in a group setting which their own conscience would normally forbid. It also explains why, in severe cases of individual superego-degradation in groups real collective mania can result, a situation in which the tension between an individual's ego and superego falls to near zero as a consequence of this process.

As our authors put it:

> For many young people the organizing strength of an ideology is necessary. They need ideas and ideals that have the power to express and to channel their unconscious stirrings, still interwoven with infantile conflicts. This task, the creation of new constructive ideals, has hardly ever been accomplished by youth alone. Ideals have always been developed over long periods of time as the result of historical evolutions and through exceptional personalities.
> Young people feel cheated by their parents without

---

[5] *Ibid.*, pp. 595–6.

really knowing of what they have been deprived. Their heroes reflect their psychological needs; disappointed by the weak father, they not only look for a strong one but try to identify with men who fulfil at the same time infantile and sadistic fantasies, such as Che Guevara or Mao Tse-tung . . .

The disappointment in the parents, the justified reproach that they do not get from the parents what they need, leads to youth's contempt of civilization, of cultural tradition, and to the opinion that there is nothing to be learned from the history of human development.[6]

Indeed, the situation is even worse than this, because as these authors also point out,

> nowadays parents anxiously try to imitate the children . . . Grownups today intrude into adolescent life by imitating their language, using their slang, dressing like them; women particularly try to affect the appearance of little girls. Aggression of the young people which does not meet with resistance leads to frustration. In vain they look for a contrast with the adult world in the family which is yielding and running after them. To block out the adults, youth is often driven to absurd behaviour and appearance.[7]

They conclude their study with these words:

> Sexual freedom has, in accordance with Freud's conception of repression, considerably transformed the manifestations of the neuroses; however, it has not produced greater mental health but only new neurotic constellations. The lesser repression of infantile sexuality has, as he feared, reduced the control of aggression. The hostility against the culture which forces the individual to restrict his libidinal and aggressive drives has grown, although the repression of drives is diminished. The task of 'reconciling men to

[6] *Ibid.*, p. 597.
[7] *Ibid.*, p. 605.

civilization' is not made easier through the liberation of drives.[8]

The works of Freud are full of warnings against the very danger which is described in the study from which I have been quoting. 'Civilization,' says Freud, 'has to be defended against the individual, and its regulations, institutions and commands are directed to that task.'[9] Speaking of the primeval events which created human society and which were summarized earlier in this book he says:

> It is in keeping with the course of human development that external coercion gradually becomes internalized: for a special mental agency, man's superego, takes it over and includes it among its commandments. Every child presents this process of transformation to us; only by that means does it become a moral and social being. Such a strengthening of the superego is a most precious cultural asset in the psychological field. Those in whom it has taken place are turned from being opponents of civilization into being its vehicles. The greater their number is in a cultural unit the more secure is its culture and the more it can dispense with external measures of coercion.[10]

It is clear that if the conclusion of the study quoted above is a reliable one then modern culture is undergoing a crisis of dissolution and decay which threatens to undermine the very foundations of social life; for the essence of the Freudian theory is that civilization is based on the superego, and if superego-formation is becoming defective then only a process of cultural degradation can result. There are many who would say that in these closing years

---

[8] Ibid., p. 607.
[9] The Future of an Illusion, XXI, p. 6.
[10] Ibid., XXI, p. 11.

of the twentieth century cultural decay and psychological degradation are to be seen all around us.

To revert to my opening discussion for a moment, one might say that the conflict between the drives of the id and the demands of the cultural superego represented above all in the taboos on incest and aggression against the father has become severely exacerbated and that, if Freud felt that in his day the balance was too far on the side of society and the superego, today it has swung too far in the direction of the individual and the id; for it is clear that a balance between these two opposing fundamental forces is the essence of human existence.

One relevant factor in this situation is the role of psychotherapy in general and of psychoanalysis in particular. As we saw, permissive trends in today's culture are in part deruved from a one-sided and shallow apprehension of Freudian ideas; but in my view the situation has not been improved by one major distortion of Freud's thinking of which many analysts and nearly all writers in the social sciences who have used psychoanalytic ideas have been guilty. This error is what might, for want of a better term, be called *the individualistic fallacy* — a methodological heresy which nicely complements the equally absurd *holistic fallacy* in the social sciences.

Some years ago I protested against the latter which, in my view, vitiates nearly all research in the so-called 'science' of sociology.[11] It is obvious that, if society is a whole greater than the sum of its individual parts, as the holistic fallacy alleges, then analysis of that social whole is impossible, and reductive, causal explanation is ruled out of court. Yet in the absence of reductive, causal explanation, holism must content itself either with an ultimate

---

[11] C. Badcock, *Lévi-Strauss*, London, 1975, pp. 26–8.

appeal to the coccult and inexplicable, or to doubtful functional metaphors concerning the 'social system', 'social organism', or whatever.

The individualistic fallacy is the exact opposite of this and is equally wrong. This holds that society is nothing more than the individuals who make it up and that they can be described, as causal agents in the social situation, solely with regard to their individual psychology and to nothing else. Sociologists have been quick to point out the obvious absurdity of this — without, of course, seeing the nonsensicality of their own position — and have rightly observed that no one is born into a vacuum, that cultures and the individuals within them vary, and that individual psychology is powerfully influenced by traditional and cultural factors of which a purely individualistic approach cannot take account. Put into precise terms, one can say that, in clinical and applied psychoanalysis, the individualistic fallacy alleges that the individual's Oedipus complex is wholly explicable by reference to himself and to his family situation, without regard to the history of that complex or to the origins of the family and of human psychological structures as a whole. Put even more succinctly, one can say that those who ignore Freud's *Totem and Taboo* — not to mention the polytraumatic theory which is being developed from it — and deny that there is any kind of archaic heritage, be it innate or acquired, commit the elementary methodological error of imagining that in every generation human psychology comes from nowhere and that the modern individual is not the product and recapitulator of the archaic past. At best they are guilty of ignoring the whole phylogenetic perspective on human psychology and, at worst, are frequently guilty of distorting, censoring and trivializing psychoanalytic insights.

Yet it is really quite obvious that the truth must lie exactly midway between these two methodological extremes: any modern psycyological event must be the product, both of contemporary psychology in individuals, and of past evolution in the species and the cultural group to which they belong. Hence the modern Oedipus complex is not wholly explicable by reference to the modern family (and therefore not controvertible by reference to modern family arrangements which allegedly do not feature it), but rather to both the individual's actual family circumstances, and to the inherited and culturally-transmitted conditions of the species which produced it in the first place and which determined its particular expression. In short, psychoanalysis must consider both ontogeny and phylogeny in coming to its conclusions. The weakness of both the holistic and individualistic approaches is that they are both in their different ways incapable of explaining the origins of phenomena; yet it is the origins which are of first importance in understanding human psychology and society. Without understanding the origins we shall make little progress in trying to comprehend the present, or indeed, any other aspect of the situation.

I propose to introduce the term *social psychoanalysis* to designate an approach to applied psychoanalysis which takes this methodological position and which therefore explains, not merely that childhood makes man, but that, because of the facts of cultural evolution briefly summarized in these pages, *man makes childhood*. Of the two perspectives, there seems little doubt that the latter is the more profound and more significant for studies in the application of psychoanalytic insights to cultural, historical and social matters. Here the individualistic, childhood-makes-man approach is relatively trivial and, paradoxically, can do little more than to complement and compound the worst aspects of the holistic fallacy by narrowly explaining adult character as a function of cultural conditioning and contemporary family circumstances.

Yet, as I pointed out above, it is the origin and causes of these circumstances which really need to be explained — not to mention other, non-individualistic phenomena like religion and cultural tradition which this approach, with its narrow focus on childhood conditioning, usually quite ignores. Social psychoanalysis, by contrast, takes the view that contemporary character should not merely be explained by reference to contemporary culture and child-rearing, but that in any society contemporary child-rearing and culture are the consequences of historical changes and that the contemporary individual recapitulates the cultural past and therefore, by a sort of reverse neoteny, experiences in his childhood the traumas and stages of ego- and superego-development which occurred in the adult lives of his ancestors. Thus cultural and psychological phylogeny complement, and are recapitulated in, individual ontogeny, just as, in the past, crucial stages in individual ontogeny became fixed as the phylogenetic heritage of subsequent generations.

Of course, Freud's own writings take both the ontogenetic and phylogenetic perspectives fully into account, and in this sense he is the true father of social psychoanalysis just as he is that of its clinical sibling. It is symptomatic of the individualistic fallacy and its popularity among therapists — who, as we shall see shortly have a special reason for embracing it — that a myth has emerged which claims that Freud himself did not take seriously his most important single work on social psychoanalysis, *Totem and Taboo*. There is no evidence for this belief except one doubtful piece of hearsay; but it is a first principle of modern reactions to Freud and psychoanalysis that facts count for nothing if the mythology is appealing enough. According to James Strachey.

> Freud himself had a very high opinion of this last essay [of *Totem and Taboo*] both as regards its content and its form.

He told his present translator [i.e., Strachey], probably in 1921, that he regarded it as his best-written work . . . the book remained a favourite all through his life and he constantly recurred to it.[12]

Freud himself said *apropos Totem and Taboo* that 'I have not written anything with so much conviction since *The Interpretation of Dreams*.'[13] At the end of his life he included a lengthy summary of the book in the equally, if not more, notorious *Moses and Monotheism* and retracted nothing of what he had said originally. Finally, in a recent conversation, Anna Freud confirmed that it always remained one of her father's favourite works and that he never doubted the correctness of its conclusions.

As far as applied psychoanalysis is concerned, the neglect of *Totem and Taboo* and Freud's phylogenetic theory in general have led to predictable consequences. The thesis which should have brought about a major revolution in the study of religion, society and culture has instead been ignored, repudiated and contradicted; the promised revolution has totally aborted and in general nothing remains in modern applied psychoanalysis of *Totem and Taboo* save an emasculated, diluted and vitiated remnant. Nevertheless, as we shall see, in analysing the cultural crisis of the twentieth century something of real significance can be achieved if we have the courage to re-instate the Freudian phylogenetic theory in its undiluted form.

As far as clinical psychoanalysts are concerned, another factor has crept into the situation. Whether these analysts commit or escape the individualistic fallacy is of little consequence because an exclusively therapeutic orientation has meant that the cultural, phylogenetic dimension of Freud's

---

[12] Introduction to *Totem and Taboo*, XIII, p. xi.

[13] E. Jones, *The Life and Work of Sigmund Freud*, New York, 1953–57, II, p. 353.

work seems of little relevance to them. One can, I think, readily see that a therapist who is exclusively concerned with individual patients and the remedying of their neurotic conflicts will tend to perceive the whole issue very much from the individual's point of view and will merely take the cultural setting as a given datum against which the neuroses of his patients are played out. Nevertheless, the fact that in recent years some clinicians have had cause to question the cultural background suggests that it can no longer be neglected. The authors of the remarkable study quoted so extensively in the first part of this chapter themselves point out that

> In a period of cultural stability, the infantile, irrational demands of the superego which conflicted with the mature superego could be worked out in the analytic process. The protecting and controlling function of the superego could be left to the influence of the surrounding society. The present cultural chaos confronts psychoanalysis with entirely new tasks. Culture is based on a balance of psychological forces and is threatened if this balance is impaired by losing one of its supports. The decline of the superego disturbs the equilibrium to a dangerous degree.[14]

The psycho-therapist, social worker or social reformer, concerned only with his own clients and their grievance against society, perhaps takes a view comparable to the private citizen of Venice who concerns himself only with the safety of his own dwelling and his own ability to get about the city. But, if the entire republic is slowly being submerged, individual citizens cannot afford to ignore their collective fate because, in the end, they all drown together if nothing is done; and again, as with Venice, what needs to be done is far beyond the powers of any one individual. In the far-from-serene republics of the modern

[14] Lowenfeld, 'Our permissive society and the superego', p. 607.

world forces are at work which threaten the entire fabric of society, and each one of us with it. In such circumstances the individual cannot think entirely of himself, and certainly the therapist can no longer afford the luxury of ignoring everything that is going on outside the consulting room; finally, in the specific circumstances of psychoanalytic theory, the individualistic fallacy can no longer go unchallenged.

4

Group Phylogeny and the Analysis of the Ego

The psychoanalytic study of childhood has established that children pass through three developmental stages: the so-called oral, anal-sadistic and phallic phases of psycho-sexual development. Reverting to my opening discussion of the evolution of the ego and superego, we can readily see the importance of these stages and we can understand why it is that the sexual drive should lend itself to such apparently irrelevant associations as the oral and anal zones. As we saw, this is the result of the fact that in human beings clearly-focused, specific sexual instincts have undergone a process of diffusion, displacement and generalization and have become associated rather more widely with the body and mind than may be true of other animals in whom these instincts still maintain a narrow and specialized role solely adapted to reproduction.

Of course, Freud, to whom we owe this discovery, did not arrive at it by way of evolutionary theory; on the contrary, he reached his conclusions by direct observation of adults and children and by a study of the psychology of human sexuality. Today, the existence of these stages of psycho-sexual development is seldom disputed, even though, as we have already seen, the full significance of infantile sexuality is characteristically denied and avoided by what might be called the modern, permissive defence

Group Phylogeny and the Analysis of the Ego

against psychoanalytic insight. Furthermore, as we shall see shortly, the individualistic fallacy obscures an obvious but usually unasked question and, in so doing, rules out of court the answer to it which, as I hope to show, solves in large measure one of the fundamental problems of the social sciences and provides us with an unparalleled insight into the social psychopathology of present-day life.

The question which tends to go unasked is this: Why do individuals go through these three stages at all, and why in that order? The reason that this question is seldom, if ever, posed like this is that the answer seems to be self-evident. The reader will probably reply that the question is quite otiose because it is obvious that, as Freud himself pointed out, the oral region is of first significance in a new-born baby's life, the anal zone is significant later, especially with the coming of toilet-training, and the phallic period is last merely because it is only later that increasing awareness of the genitals and the ability to manipulate them and perceive the persons of the parents causes Oedipal phenomena (which are synonymous with the phallic period) to come to the fore.

All this is, of course, perfectly true. But, in reply, let me make two fundamental points which, I think, make the original question far from otiose and the answer to it anything but platitudinous.

My first point is that, although the three developmental stages, oral–anal–phallic, are universal, they are not of the same universal significance in all societies. The research of Geza Roheim, summarized in my *Psycho-analysis of Culture*, shows quite clearly that the oral period, for instance, does not have the same significance for Australian aborigine hunter-gatherers as it does for Melanesian agriculturalists; and further that, in the former instance, the anal-sadistic hardly seems to exist (with the consquent absence of sado-masochistic perversions or character traits in adults). Now, this clearly calls for comment. Why is it that in some societies like our own the three stages of childhood development are clearly distinguishable and of great importance as far as personality formation is concerned, whereas in other societies this is much less true, and one or two stages seem to be almost absent altogether? Furthermore, as we shall see, the latency period, which follows these three stages as another developmental marker, is certainly not universal in its cultural aspects even if, as we noted earlier, basic neuro-physiological phenomena related to latency are. This clearly demands an answer, and it is one which the individualistic, myopically-therapeutic psychoanalysis of the present cannot supply.

My second point is more subtle, but equally pertinent. Although the sequence oral–anal–phallic seems to be, and indeed is, determined by the basic pattern of infantile physical development—oral dependence giving way to increasing control of the anal sphincter, followed by development of genital sensitivity, etc. — the pattern of instinctual renunciation and control which this series represents is derived from another, different series in which the stages originally occurred in a different order.

To understand why this is so we need to return to the polytrauma theory outlined earlier and see what its significance is for the development of the modern individual.

It was argued earlier that man, a creature with unprepossessing qualities for higher social development, became capable of that development because of traumatic social changes which occurred in the past but whose impact was so immense that they have shaped human nature down to the present and have been the determining influences on the evolution of culture, whose function, by and large, is the transmission of the consequences of these primal, traumatic experiences to subsequent generations in the form of ego, and, most especially, superego, development. We saw that the first, and most important, of these traumatic social changes was the transition from vegetarian foraging to big-game hunting which precipitated the murder of the primal father, and that subsequent totemic culture, still extant until recently in some parts of the world, was a consequence of this. We saw that initiation ceremonies and totemic ceremonial in general were means of instilling in fresh generations the consequences of the traumatic experiences of their predecessors. Later, it was argued that the coming of cultivation meant another, although admittedly much less traumatic change, and resulted in weaning becoming established as a major and most significant developmental stage. As we saw, the consequences of this change, and individuals' response to the much more disciplinarian and dominant mothers who brought it about, gave rise to the elaborate symbolism and religious ritual of early polytheism (including matters which there was not the opportunity to mention, such as the Neolithic enthusiasm for ritual burial in Mother Earth, frequently in a foetal position[1]). But already we can see one most unexpected and surprising consequence of this: if what we may call the phallic or Oedipal trauma came first in human cultural history and was the original event from which all else flowed, then in terms of individual psychosexual development it follows last, preceded by the oral stage whose cultural equivalent succeeded it!

In fact, that situation is even more confusing than it may seem from this account because a third cultural trauma, this time representing the change from cultivation (of plants) to herding and pastoralism also occurred and brought with it a great intensification, not of weaning as happened with cultivation, nor of the phallic mutilations which accompanied hunting, but of toilet-training. The

[1] J. Hawkes, and L. Wolley, *The History of Mankind*, New York, 1963, I, p. 341.

justification for this perhaps surprising proposition is not merely that pastoral peoples do in fact show a fastidiousness with regard to the excremental functions which is totally unknown among primeval hunter-gatherers and rarely seen among agriculturalists (although in their case the situation is complicated by subsequent introduction of domesticated animals), but that toilet-training and the mastery of the anal sphincter is, as we know from observation of our own children, intimately involved with sadistic instinctual trends and consists in the child accepting self-censorship of his anal and excremental drives. By contrast to weaning, which represents the loss of a love-object (the breast) and which produces a characteristic culturally valued response (mastery of the ability to postpone oral gratification in the interests of agriculture), toilet-training represents a more-or-less voluntary submission to an educative influence and a partial redirection against the self of the sadistic drive which is associated with the anal function. This phenomenon of mastery of the anal drive turns out to be of the first importance for pastoral peoples because, as I have demonstrated elsewhere,[2] pastoral psychology is often based on the introjection of sadistic drives which would otherwise threaten the herds on which the pastoralist depends for his existence. Thus, in a thoroughly typical way, man, who is not endowed with an instinctive love of animals or care for them, achieves the ability to make a success of animal-husbandry as a form of economic life by channelling his otherwise rampant aggressiveness back against himself as a force of conscience which frequently expresses itself in pastoral cultures as a vengeful and recriminating god of the sky. The pastoralist who can control his aggression with regard to his animals has in his childhood first had to learn how to do it with regard to his excremental activities and the parental

[2] *The Psychoanalysis of Culture*, pp. 101–21.

authority-figures who insisted on this first essential moulding of his character. If, by way of consequence, our pastoralist who is punctilious about his execretory functions also develops a characteristic personality trait — the compulsion to hard wealth — then this will be all the better for his herds which, in a non-monetary economy, are the equivalent of capital.

Returning now to our basic theory, we see that the extension of Freud's monotraumatic theory of human social evolution to a polytraumatic one allows us to discern in human cultural evolution a pattern which, if it should prove to be real, may perhaps represent for the human sciences something like the revolution introduced into the physical sciences by Copernicus, Kepler and Galileo. Now we can begin to see the outlines of a theory of human personality and cultural development which is elegant indeed and which reduces to a few general principles many of the random and apparently unsystematic motions of human history and culture. We see that we have three social revolutions of decreasing traumatic intensity, each representing an economic and cultural advance and each providing the basis for one of the modern stages of individual psychosexual development. First comes the collective phallic or Oedipal trauma described in *Totem and Taboo*. It is a trauma concerning competition against the father for the possession of the mother and culminates in the suppression of the phallic or genital drive by the taboo on incest and parricide. In the race this is the original social and psychological trauma which makes civilized society possible and which produces as its embodiment totemic religion. In the individual it is the culmination of childhood psychosexual development and produces — or should produce — the resolution of the Oedipus complex and provides the totemic parallel of childhood, the animal phobia, and the equivalent in adult psychopathology, the anxiety hysteria. Next comes the oral trauma associated with the coming of weaning and agriculture and resulting in polytheistic relgion. This is perpetuated in modern weaning during the oral stage and finds an equivalent in manic-depressive and paranoid-schizophrenic disorders. Finally, we have a cultural anal trauma associated with pastoralism and monotheism whose modern adult equivalent is obsessional neurosis and whose pre-Oedipal focus lies in the anal-sadistic phase.

We are now in a position to answer the question with which we started: namely, why do individuals in our culture go through these three stages of developmental growth in the manner in which they do? The answer is now clear, and it is far from platitudinous; indeed, as we shall see in the next chapter, it is fundamental to an understanding of the modern world. The answer is that individuals have to develop like this because we live in societies which have evolved through all three stages of economic and cultural adaptation (and their frequent partial repetitions and recapitulations). Therefore individuals need to possess personalities conformable to the ambient level of cultural evolution. This demands that they each individually recapitulate within their own personal development the evolution of their culture — a process which is the unconscious and fundamental equivalent of formal education. An individual in our culture needs to be weaned and to experience the loss of the breast because we live in societies based on agriculture and requiring an ability to postpone immediate instinctual gratification. Secondly, an individual needs to undergo toilet-training not merely because of the demands of common decency and modern personal hygiene, but, much more importantly, because we live in a culture in which an ability to control sadistic drives is of the first importance, both for the quality of our civilization and for the acquisition and protection of our cultural wealth in general. Lastly, individuals in our culture, as in all others, must respect the two basic prohibitions on which all human societies are founded: that forbidding murder of our fellow men and that forbidding the erotic drives which give rise to the wish to murder in its most elemental instance — parricide for possession of the mother.

If my readers still doubt this let them consider the situation as we find it among societies which have not advanced as far as we have, for instance, among the aborigines of Central Australia. In this case we find a culture which has not evolved beyond the initial, hunter-gatherer stage and which, furthermore, does not appear to have been contaminated by contact with cultures which had done so — at least, until the coming of white men. This is also one of those cultures in which the relative absence of the latency period is alleged to disprove the Freudian theory of child development. As we shall see, it does no such thing.

Because the Australian aborigines still exist at the hunter-gatherer level of culture they have no need for a weaning trauma in early childhood as is found among all primitive agriculturalists, and consequently children, although experiencing a period of oral dependency as they do in the West, linger in that stage, do not have to give it up and, in a sense, remain unweaned until adulthood — or, certainly until initiation, which is essentially the same thing. Indeed, Roheim reports that mothers will never deny the breast to a child of any age, even to save a younger one from starvation; and a child who for some reason cannot nevertheless find the mother's breast can usually find another woman ready to suckle him.[3] In these societies the mother *is* the breast — passive, all-giving, exploited and totally non-disciplinarian. In childhood children run wild, are subject to little or no educative influence and are generally indulged. What is true of oral instinctual drives is also true of anal and genital ones. There is no

---

[3] Roheim, *Psychoanalysis and Anthropology*, pp. 55–6.

attempt to toilet-train children whatsoever and so consequently adults and children will by and large relieve themselves wherever and whenever they feel the need to do so. (Not surprisingly, constipation is virtually unknown and purgatives never resorted to. Yet in many pastoral societies, and in the modern West and Japan, they are widely used, in some of the former instances becoming virtual panaceas.) Again, infantile masturbation and other sexual practices are tolerated — even regarded as amusing by adults — and certainly are not prohibited or censored. Only observation of parental intercourse is prohibited — a very significant exception in the light of basic psychoanalytic theory — but as these people sleep in the open around camp-fires and children can easily feign sleep, this rule is unenforceable.

However, at initiation, as we have already seen, all this changes. It is almost as if all the punishment, admonishment and educative pressure which the aboriginal child has been spared up to this moment is suddenly and simultaneously inflicted on him (here, for once, the masculine pronoun does not embrace the feminine because initiation is an exclusively masculine affair). Now a boy becomes instantly weaned because he would not dream of sucking at his mother's breast now that he is a man. Again, now that he is a man he is expected to observe those admittedly very minimal standards of decency which apply to excretion (for instance, not urinating on somone's feet when you are talking to them), and so to this very limited extent we can speak of initiation being like toilet-training. Most important of all, the cultural prohibitions on his genital urge are now fully enforced and he must give up the freedom of infantile sexual gratification for the responsibilities of adult life; in short, he must obey the taboos against incest embodied in the elaborate kinship systems of the Australian aborigines and observe those against parricide enshrined in the totemic religion.

Now we can readily see that the evident lack of a culturally defined latency period — by which we really mean one resulting from an enforcement of the incest taboo during childhod — is entirely explicable and, indeed, inevitable in these circumstances. Because the phallic stage of sexual development continues for the Australian aborigines right up to puberty and because resolution of the Oedipus complex cannot occur until initation, it follows as a matter of inexorable logic that a latency period recognizable as a consequence of a culturally induced culmination of the Oedipal stage cannot be expected. The fact that this is indeed found to be the case powerfully corroborates the theory of development being advanced in these pages and demonstrates that the apparent absence of the latency phenomenon as we know it among primitive people like the Australian aborigines is no proof of the falsity of the idea of latency as such. On the contrary, it completely vindicates it. (I am of course ignoring here the question of the neuro-physiological maturation underlying the development of ego-functions at about the age of seven which was discussed above (see p. 33–4). This is probably true of all human beings irrespective of culture and simply means that some degree of maturation of the ego must occur at around the age of seven even if the culture does not choose that moment for the installation of the superego. The reader will recall that latency in this genetically determined, physiological sense is a consequence of neoteny, itself the cause of the postponement of sexual maturity until adolescence which is a contributory, but not a necessary or determining, cause of the resolution of the Oedipus complex which in our culture should normally usher in the latency period.)

Before we leave this discussion of basic theory and turn our attention finally to the modern world, there is one further point that I think is worth making and that is part of the answer to the second question asked above, namely, why do individuals go through the three stages in the conventional order?

We have already seen that the answer is the obvious one that the sequence oral–anal–phallic is determined in the main by developmental physiology. But we have also seen that in the species the order of the corresponding stages of cultural development was different: phallic–oral–anal.[4] It now remains to ask whether there is any significance in this hitherto unknown fact.

Put in terms of basic psychoanalytic theory, one might say that in the modern Western individual the order of stages of psycho-sexual development has been determined by the id. The stages of cultural development, however, represent not merely a sequence of economic and social advances, but also of psychological ones. The agency implicated in these is clearly not the id, nor simply the ego, but rather the superego. What this means in the most simple terms is that the order of onset of the stages in the individual is determined by what occasions them as gratifications — the oral stage by suckling, the anal by evacuating solid matter, the phallic by experiencing genital, Oedipal excitement. The cultural order of stages, however, is determined by the sequence in which these gratifications were frustrated and subjected to inhibition. The practical result of this is that when we study the individual child we see a succession of stages of development which from the point of view of the id are just as

---

[4] At the time of writing *The Psychoanalysis of Culture* the elegant theory outlined in these pages was not fully clear to me and I committed the understandable, but crude, error of assuming that individual psychological ontogeny recapitulates collective psychological phylogeny *in the same order of stages*. Clearly this is not so; and thus the theory advanced in that book must be modified to include the important correction contained in this.

they should be and — because the id is the oldest, most fundamental and, from the point of view of the instinctual drives which originate it, the most important agency — are just what they should be. But if we then turn to the ego — and, still more, the superego — and try to understand the sequence of development there we may find ourselves in the predicament of a person who tried to investigate the musical education of a child who had started learning the piano with grade 2, then gone on to grade 3, and finally ended with grade 1! Such a distorted sequence might have profound effects on the student's musical abilities, especially in the earlier stages, and would certainly make the pedagogic method seem problematic to anyone who did not know that the order of grades had been transposed. It is just possible that this is exactly the situation that we face when, as individuals, we experience these stages, and it may certainly be the situation that, as psychoanalysts, we encounter when we try to reconstruct the phases of ego- and superego-development from the sole evidence of the clinical analysis of individuals (For instance, I strongly suspect that this fact has seriously misled the Kleinian school in its theory of developmental stages and is still obscuring much of the psychological structure of the psychoses, and perhaps the neuroses too.)

Like the reader who finds that the chapters of his detective novel have been printed in the wrong order, we may only now be beginning to understand why from the point of view of ego- and superego-development the crime which should be at the beginning (that of Oedipus) comes at the end, and why what comes at the beginning (the oral period) leads unintelligibly into what should otherwise have been the conclusion of the story (anal stage, latency)! At the very least, this raises some important questions for ego-psychology and indicates what Freud — but few others since — always knew, namely, that group- and ego-psychology are deeply and intimately intertwined.

And, if the situation with regard to individual psychological development and the evolution of culture is as I have represented it, then this is merely the first of many profound insights into the psychology of the ego — and perhaps most especially the superego — which can be expected but which were totally unobtainable as long as the individualistic fallacy blocked the way. As will be seen in my concluding remarks, there are some reasons for believing that the era of a true psychoanalytic psychology of the superego is about to dawn.

5

The Psychopathology of Present-day Life

If, bearing in mind the theory of society and superego development so far advanced in this book, we now turn our attention back to the analysis of modern culture outlined in the article from which I quoted so extensively in the chapter before last, we can see that the following remarks, also from that article, take on a much greater significance in the light of the point which I made at the conclusion of the last regarding the lack of a culturally determined latency period among the Australian aborigines:

> Another consequence of the changed upbringing is a less marked latency period in many children. Freud emphasized the importance of the latency period for the cultural development of the individual, and hence the society. He pointed out that the latency period is absent in primitive societies and is found only in higher cultures.[1]

But what is the fate of a higher culture like ours in which the latency period does not develop as it should and in which, consequently, the Oedipal dilemma is not satisfactorily resolved? The authors give an answer based on their own case material:

[1] Lowenfeld, 'Our permissive society and the superego', p. 594.

unresolved oedipal problems (which formerly might have produced a typical hysteria) may today lead to a state of unrestrained and self-destructive acting out, and to delinquency, simulating a picture of psychosis, as the ego remains weak and the superego ineffectual in the face of uncontrolled drives.[2]

Commenting on a study which they made in 1965 of applications for treatment at the New York Psychoanalytic Institute, they find the following typical pattern:

> the oedipus complex is not fully resolved; the superego, incompletely developed, cannot sufficiently support the weak ego. The social superego is also ineffectual and its representatives give no support. Thus the ego is not capable of successful integration with the other components of the psychic apparatus. The individual gains no narcissistic gratification from his ego ideal. His affects are governed by guilt feelings, not accessible to his conscious mind. Here we have a repetition of the childhood in which the parent's weakness contributed to the unconscious need for punishment.[3]

The relevance of the lengthy preliminary exposition which I devoted to the modern Freudian theory of society should now begin to become apparent. It should become clear that this lessening of the prevalence and importance of the latency period in modern Western societies is a social symptom of the first diagnostic importance. Like the absence of dilation in the pupils following a head-injury, this apparently small, perhaps even seemingly trivial, symptom turns out to be of crucial importance. But, of course, such slight diagnostic indications mean little unless a theory is to hand which can explain their crucial

---

[2] *Ibid.*, pp. 601–2.
[3] *Ibid.*, p. 599.

importance. If it were not known that pupil-dilation was intimately related to neurological functioning of the brain its absence in some cases of head injury might go unremarked; but once its significance is appreciated, such a seemingly slight symptom assumes drastic importance. So it is with the latency phenomenon. Its lessening and perhaps even virtual disappearance in some cases as a culturally-marked developmental period is of the first importance and is one of the most disquieting symptoms of modern social change.

It is clear that if the theory of social evolution briefly summarized in these pages is correct, then this is not how it should be. We saw earlier that, following the Neolithic Revolution, child-rearing regimes assumed an importance which they have never lost in all human cultures based on agriculture and more advanced modes of economic life. Central to child-rearing from the cultural point of view, as we have seen, is that by the time he is six or seven the child should have been able to recapitulate within his own personal psychological development the development history of his culture. The reader will recall that I argued that this meant satisfactorily surmounting the three stages of psychosexual growth which psychoanalysis discovered long ago to be typical of most individuals in our culture.

Yet the data described by the survey of the New York Psychoanalytic Institute mentioned above show that in a significant number of cases such patterns of personal development are no longer occurring. If this is indeed so, and if it is true that the latency period is in decline as an important cultural phenomenon, then it seems difficult not to conclude that in some very significant respects modern Western child-rearing practices are approximating more to those of pre-Neolithic, pre-agricultural societies like those of the Australian aborigines than to modern industrial ones. The study from which I am quoting reinforces this conclusion when it comments that:

In large parts of the population there is little discipline over the pregenital, and particularly the oral, drives of children. The aggressive drives meet with weak control. Television, itself a constant passive-oral indulgence, stimulates and satisfies sadistic fantasies; at the same time it blunts responsiveness to one's sadistic impulses. Here are the roots of the regressive trends in adolescence and in adult life.[5]

But modern industrial societies are in some respects in a worse position than the hunter-gatherer societies to which such relatively defective ego and superego development is normal, because they lack any institutional means of correcting the situation at puberty. Whereas, as we have seen, primal societies use the initiation and totemic rituals to instil whatever rudimentary superego-formation is necessary for the conduct of their social life, modern societies have more or less totally abandoned these rituals and anything resembling them (although vestiges of them can still be found in some educational and penal institutions). Indeed, if anything, modern societies seem bent on compounding the problem by considerably lengthening and complicating adolescence — a period of life which, as we have seen, barely exists in totemic societies where individuals go from childhood to adulthood via a few days of traumatic initiation. Considering all this, then, it is not surprising that so many of today's adolescents seem to experience great difficulty in maturing:

> Society has also developed a new attitude toward pregenital drives, which are given a special value and are highly esteemed. Whereas formerly only a few writers (such as de Sade and Sacher-Masoch) propagated their practice, today they play a decisive role in our culture, literature, art, music, theater and movies. The freedom in the growing up of the child allows a fixation to the pre-

[4] *Ibid.*, pp. 593–4.

genital phase and facilitates regression to it. Today many young people fail in the task of maturing into the genital phase of adolescence, a process which apparently needs much time; they do not fully outgrow the phallic stage.[5]

A failure to reach the genital stage in adolescence is, of course, a consequence of failure to resolve the Oedipus complex satisfactorily.

An inability to mature adequately out of the phallic, Oedipal phase will usually not only result in some degree of genital inhibition later in life and a fixation on infantile sexual gratifications such as masturbation, voyeurism, sado-masochism, etc., but also reduce the force of the cultural prohibitions which the original phallic-Oedipal trauma of our forefathers precipitated, namely those against parricide and incest. Indeed, since this trauma was the origin of all later stages of cultural evolution for the race as a whole and is now the culminating phase of childhood development, it is clear that on this phase more than any other the whole mental health and normality not only of the individual, but of the society, depends. This is why success in surmounting this stage in a satisfactory manner is so important both for the happiness and future sexual fulfilment of the individual and for the security and success of this civilization.

Put another way, and in Freud's own words, we can say that 'the superego is stunted in its strength and growth if the surmounting of the Oedipus complex is only incompletely successful.' He continues to add that 'In the course of development the superego also takes on the influences of those who have stepped into the place of parents — Educators, teachers, people chosen as ideal models.'[6] But in this respect too there is good reason to believe that things have recently begun to go seriously wrong:

[5] *Ibid.*, p. 606.
[6] *New Introductory Lectures on Psychoanalysis*, XXII, p. 64.

The youth of today are being deserted by their parents in regard to the superego development. The ego alone — particularly when not strengthend in the upbringing — can hardly solve the taks of control and sublimation. Parents seem to have abdicated; schools and colleges also fail in this task.[7]

Whereas in the past such external supports of the superego might have been strong enough to compensate at least in part for faulty superego development as a result of difficulties at the phallic-Oedipal stage and might have contributed to the unresolved Oedipal conflict expressing itself as a typical hysteria or obsessional neurosis, today, because such supports are in large part lacking, the outcome is not likely to be the same. On the contrary, we have already seen that according to modern studies of the problem 'unrestrained and self-destructive acting out' and 'delinquency, simulating a picture of psychosis'[8] are in fact more likely. As we shall see later, it is not that the superego does not exist in these circumstances, but that it is undeveloped, unsupported by cultural forces of a progressive character (and therefore vulnerable to exploitation by those of a regressive nature), and is primitive in its functioning. But whereas neurosis is, in a sense, a private affair, affecting mainly the person who suffers from it, delinquency and acting-out of neurotic conflicts are much more the concern of society as a whole and are certainly likely to affect others to a greater degree than is normally true of the symptoms of a conventional neurosis. Here we have another instance of the need to transcend a narrowly individualistic approach to modern psychopathology: the question of the social and cultural consequences of failure satisfactorily to resolve the Oedipus complex in the context of modern culture.

[7] Lowenfeld, 'Our permissive society and the superego', p. 597.
[8] Ibid., pp. 601–2 and pp. 102–3.

If we now turn to a consideration of the social consequences of failure at the phallic stage of Oedipal resolution combined with inadequate superego-development and regressive fixations, we will see that all forms of behaviour which represent aggression directed at the father are the consequence of the fundamental failure to renounce the mother as a love-object. This is simply the modern individual equavialent of the psychoanalytic principle which holds that primal parricide was a consequence of a desire for incest with the mother. As long as a son holds on to the mother as a love-object he must ineluctably be in conflict with the father, just as, conversely, as soon as he accepts the paternal authority and identifies with his father to constitute his superego he must suppress his fundamental parricidal antagonism and with it his incestuous fixation.

Although such an incestuous fixation usually means genital inhibition for the individual in adult life, resulting either in perversion or neurosis or both and invariably in some unhappiness, incest in itself does not threaten the foundations of culture so much as the consequent erotic and aggressive antagonism to which it gives rise. Indeed, we saw at the beginning that this was the principal reason for culture in the first place: it was a means of containing such anti-social antagonisms in what was, for a gelada-like hominid, a novel mode of subsistence which demanded considerable social cooperation, altruism and restraint. But what was true of the beginnings of human culture is still true today, and it seems that much in modern society can be understood as reflecting just such a parricidal, antagonistic and regressive trend. The ever-rising statistics of delinquency and crime, and particularly violent crime, probably result in large part from a failure to establish the paternal authority in childhood and with it the normal, positive resolution of the Oedipus complex which it produces. Furthermore, the fact that so much violent crime is committed by the younger generation — the modern equivalent of the sons of the primal father — certainly seems to point to a fundamental failure in socialization or, in other words, in superego-formation. In social symptoms like these we have evidence of one of the most basic and dangerous erosions of all — that of the basic psychological restraints against the war of all against all (and especially of sons against fathers) which threatens to erupt once the fundamental processes of socialization begin to break down. It would appear that if present trends like these continue unchecked the future can only bring increasing social disintegration, mounting crime, delinquency and violence, and decreasing safety and security of life, particularly for the weak and unprotected. If the absolutely fundamental achievements of human culture represented in the prohibitions on violence against authority and the temptation to incest which occasion it are loosened, then we stand at the edge of a frightful abyss which represents a collapse into an almost pre-human state of savagery and violence. Whether such a prognosis is indeed likely or not is a question to which we shall return shortly, but for the time being let us merely note the danger, which is in any event a very real one, and pass on.

Because the father is the model for the superego and the actual embodiment of authority and the demands of the cultural prohibitions against incest and parricide within the individual's own family, it is perhaps not surprising that the antagonism towards him and what he stands for need not be limited to such self-evidently anti-social and aggressive tendencies as those revealed in the statistics of crime and violence. Hatred of the father expresses itself not only in obvious antagonistic behaviour directed at all representatives of paternal restraint, but also in more devious and perhaps even 'sublimated' ways as a distaste for all restraints of any kind and an opposition to authority of any sort. The sociologist Bernice Martin has perceptively summed up the situation in terms of recent English culture when she says that:

The most salient feature of the counter-culture of the 1960s was the symbolism of anti-structure. It was essentially a pitting of freedom and fluidity against form and structure. Sixties expressiveness was a long and concerted attack on boundaries, limits, certainties, conventions, taboos, roles, system, style, category, predictability, form, structure and ritual.[9]

In short, an attack on all cultural derivations of the censoring, criticizing, evaluating superego and, fundamentally, an assault on its most precious and primitive prohibition, that against incest — the ultimate limit, barrier and restraint both for the individual and the culture. What Bernice Martin terms the 'Expressive Revolution' was in reality the cultural expression of defective superego-formation of epidemic proportions and chronic irresolution at the Oedipal stage of development in a vociferous fraction of the modern population, especially the young. One of the most bizarre examples of this 'Expressive Revolution' occurred (under my own eyes as it happened) at the London School of Economics during one of the frequent student occupations. Bernice Martin describes it as follows:

> The students not only tore down the separate 'Ladies' and 'Gentlemen' notices from the lavatories . . . but they even painted out the distinction between first floor and second, between second and third and so on: even purely functional classifications of space had to go, jut as the watches and clocks had to be discarded in order to free time.[10]

The fact that such an 'Expressive Revolution' is not unrelated to other, much more obviously parricidal ones, and that all of these insurrections against cultural restraint can be traced to childhood failures in the acquisition of the

[9] *A Sociology of Contemporary Cultural Change*, Oxford, 1981, p. 25.
[10] Ibid., p. 205.

superego is nicely illustrated by an Italian terrorist who, having put his revolutionary ideology into practice by murdering seventeen people and kidnapping an American general, justified his activities at his trial by proudly explaining that 'My challenge began from the school benches of Centocelle [his home town]. We felt the need to struggle to conquer new space and not be crushed by rules . . . .'[11]

Although — most fortunately — not everybody who feels the need to assert themselves against rules becomes a mass-murderer, there is undoubtedly today a widespread feeling that all rules and regulations are onerous and provocative. It is almost as if the modern mind, unable to tolerate cultural restraints, and feeling that discontent in civilization which Freud described long ago, had become so intolerant of the demands of communal existence and civilized behaviour that it saw each and every representative of those restraints as an incitement to revolt rather in the same way that an enraged revolutionary mob, thirsting for the blood of its oppressors, might fall on some unfortunate bystander merely because he happened to bear a resemblance to the head of the secret police. Indeed, during a summer of rioting by juvenile delinquents in England recently in the course of which whole urban areas were terrorized, looted and in some cases burnt to the ground, it was seriously suggested that the police had been to blame merely by being there to enforce the law. Their presence was said to have been 'provocative'; but provocative of what? Presumably of law-breaking and attacks on themselves, because this is what the allegation of 'provocation' was used to excuse. Yet anyone who wishes to understand the latent determinants of human behaviour would be unwise to reject this excuse as totally false. It contains a major element of truth, even if it is not precisely

[11] *The Times*, 8 May 1982.

the truth which its originators intended. There is a real element of truth in it if we conclude, as I think we must, that in those who have failed to come to terms with the demands of a civilized existence any representative of that existence can be seen as an incitement to protest, especially if, as in the case of the police, that representative has only too obvious a resemblance to the forbidding father of early childhood with whom the individual has not come to terms because of chronic irresolution of the Oedipal dilemma. Thus, in the sense that jewellers who keep valuable items in their shop-windows cause smash-and-grab raids and women who walk alone cause rapes, it may be said that the police do, in a sense, cause riots and lawbreaking merely by existing.

Indeed, so profound and all-pervading is the modern resentment of authority, restraint and control in all its forms that even types of protest which seem to be motivated by the highest ideals of civilized behaviour and the most tender manifestations of conscience can be shown to originate in it. I can speak authoritatively on one form of resentment of authority which I have had to get to know — albeit unwillingly — in intimate detail: the student protest movement. Happening by chance to be employed in one of the most notoriously protest-prone university schools in the Western world, I have noticed an extraordinary anomaly in student protest behaviour which I invite my readers to compare with their own experience, which I think they will find quite closely comparable to my own. They will find that student protesters are extremely discriminating about what they protest against. In theory, the student protester will say that he is against any and all instances of injustice, inhumanity, exploitation, colonialism, violence, limitation of freedom of speech, or whatever (the list is a long one!). Yet, in practice, students in Western countries only protest about these things if they can detect them in their own, or allied, cultures. Geographical distance is no bar — they will, for instance, happily protest about the doings of governments or individuals on the other side of the world, but only if those governments or individuals are white, European in culture and committed to liberal democracy. If they should chance to be black, brown or yellow, of any cultural tradition save that of the West and dominated by any other ideological system except that of the student's own parents they will seldom if ever protest, no matter how flagrant the injustice, how onerous the oppression, how unprincipled the exploitation and how ever much they offend against the protesters' vociferously expressed and allegedly 'sincere' ideals. Yet an individual or government possessing the qualifications of being white, European in cultural origin and liberal-democratic by conviction will be remorselessly and unreasonably criticized for each and every offence against the supposedly absolute standards of protest-morality. In the event of both protagonists in a conflict being identifiable with the wrong — that is, with the parental — values, the protagonist who most closely approximates to them will be protested against and the other, no matter how objectively wrong they may be, will be totally vindicated and absolutely right.

In the latter case, of course, the sole criterion for being in the right is that of being opposed to the protagonist most closely identified with the parental authority — a very easy requirement to fulfil as the following true, but rather ludicrous, example shows. At the time of writing, a South American military dictatorship, in clear violation of all internation law and morality, invaded a British dependency and subjected its citizens to humiliating and oppressive military rule. Up until this point the military dictatorship in question had been an archetypal target for student protesters who expressed total solidarity with the left-wing guerillas who opposed it. Taking the radical students' ideals at face-value one might have expected

The Psychopathology of Present-day Life 101

them to see this incident as yet another example of oppression by a fascist regime and protest against it — after all, they protested enough when it used such methods against its own people. But the moment the military dictatorship resorted to armed aggression against British subjects the radical student protester, who cared for nothing but his ideals and for justice, freedom and equality, unhesitatingly sided with the invaders and began to protest, not against them, but against his own government's attempts to restore the freedom, democratic rights and civil liberty of those who had lost them!

This example, and many others which I am sure my readers can supply from their own experience, clearly reveals the true nature of student and much other protest. It is in fact directed against the protesters' own parents — especially the father — and is intended to take the place of the infantile and adolescent reproaches and criticisms of the parental authority which have now come to be directed at each and any cultural equivalent of the father. This explains why heads of governments, the police and the Establishment in general are such popular targets for the protesters' attacks. Fundamentally, such protests against the cultural surrogates of the parents arise from the same origin as the assault on boundaries, standards and restraints — the parricidal resentment against the father's sexual rights over the mother which results from the failure to resolve the Oedipal conflict. Protest, to model a phrase on Clausewitz, seems to be the continuation of the Oedipus complex by other means.

Another amusing, but really quite typical example which transparently reveals the father-protest behind all other protests is provided by one of the cases cited in the study from which I have already quoted at length:

> the boy joined a Communist youth group, became more masculine and energetic, and participated in protest mar-

ches and picketing and even dared to wear the party button in school. However, when his father confided in him that he too was a Communist, the interest in the cause dwindled, and the boy soon exchanged the party button for a series of buttons with obscene words . . .

One can speculate that this boy might some day join one of the rebellious students who fight the establishment in an astonishingly infantile way, expecting at the same time not to be punished and to be granted full amnesty for their transgressions, just as a small child would expect from an indulgent parent.[12]

Let us return for a moment to the question of prognosis: what can be the outcome for modern societies of the phenomenon which we have been discussing? One possibility that has already been mentioned is anarchy, a progressive collapse of the social order because of the failure of the superego mechanisms which underpin it. Yet, as we have seen, things might not be so simple. It may be that even though certain aspects of the superego do not develop, other, different ones might do so instead; or it might be that, in the absence of a superego which forbids parricide and incest, an individual might develop some other kind of superego with other, perhaps analogous prohibitions. Whether such prohibitions would meet the requirements of the situation as far as society is concerned is a moot point, but it is worth considering. Certainly, we might be justified in assuming that whatever kind of superego a person had it might have some controlling, drive-inhibiting aspects, and consequently that anarchy, which is equivalent to a more or less complete absence of controls, is an unlikely outcome. In any case, social prognosis is a notoriously unsafe activity, and it is one from which we might wisely refrain.

[12] Lowenfeld, 'Our permissive society and the superego', pp. 602–3.

Nevertheless, the question still remains as to whether there is more to the situation than a simple failure in superego-development and a consequent antagonism towards all forms of authority and restraint. If we return, for example, to the case of student protesters, we have already noted that they show some signs of a need for parental surrogates, and certainly they are seldom complete anarchists. On the contrary, they usually give strong support to social institutions such as trade unions, radical political parties or government agencies whose activities they approve. Indeed, one often gets the feeling that these young people have a positive need for a disciplining, controlling and directing father-figure, but that the father-figures they want are not the ones they have.

This need for the father probably goes back to an earlier stage of childhood than the phallic-Oedipal one to which we have so far confined our attention. We have already seen that failure satisfactorily to surmount the Oedipus complex results in pre-Oedipal fixations, notably at the anal and oral stages, and it may be here that we can find the primitive, rudimentary superego elements which can, and indeed must, remain when the mature superego does not develop. In particular, it is not difficult to imagine that the oral stage, with its central feature of attachment to the breast, and thereby to the person of the mother, holds rich possibilities for primitive superego-formation, especially if weaning creates a tendency to introject the lost object. Furthermore, this is probably one of those cases where social psychoanalysis can succeed in telling us more about this primitive superego-structure than can the clinical analysis of modern individuals unaided by cultural insights. This is partly because, as indicated earlier, the acquisition of the superego takes place in the modern individual in a different sequence of stages than it did in the culture, and partly because cultural psychological phenomena often present a clearly separated-out picture of their components whereas individual neuroses are often less easy to disentangle. In the latter case one is confronted by something like a functioning assembly which needs to be dismantled and analysed before it can be understood, whereas in the former case one has something much more like an 'exploded' view of things as seen in a working-drawing. Certainly, the social psychoanalysis of the oral aspects of the cultural superego seems far easier than the corresponding attempts to analyse pre-Oedipal oral superego elements in the development of the child where the crucial phenomena have occurred long before the acquisition of language, and where analytic 'reconstructions' are more likely to reflect the theoretical expectations of the analyst than they do the reality.[13] Let us therefore review what we learnt earlier about the cultural oral superego — the mother goddess, in other words — and see what significance it has for our problem.

We saw in regard to the coming of agriculture that the introduction of weaning produced reactions in early agricultural populations which are detectable in their religious, literary and mythical culture. One aspect of this which, as I pointed out, is in fact first seen in late Palaeolithic delayed-return hunter-gatherer cultures, is the appearance of the cult of the all-providing and divinely-fecund mother-goddess — the phantasied mother-as-breast. This epiphany of the mother of the immediate-return hunter-gatherers — or of the new-born and unweaned child, which is the same thing — was clearly designed to compensate for her loss in reality. Human culture, which at this period was making its first faltering steps towards thorough-going agriculturalism and the full-scale Neolithic Revolution which it was to bring in its train,

[13] K. R. Eissler, 'Irreverent remarks about the present and the future of psychoanalysis', *International Journal of Psychoanalysis* 50 (1969), p. 462, quoting Anna Freud's 1967 Freud Anniversary Lecture.

seems to have found the loss of the ur-mother of the primal hunting and gathering society hard to get over. Although the figure of the earth-mother pales in time (receiving a last fitful refulgence in the West in 1950 when she was proclaimed bodily assumed into heaven by Pope Pius XII), she nevertheless remained a permanent part of the polytheistic pantheons which evolved first of all during the Neolithic period.

In the modern individual such a clearly defined and providential maternal version of the superego does not appear to emerge in quite the same way during and after the oral period, almost certainly because in individual history, unlike that of the culture, the oral period does not follow Oedipal resolution and therefore cannot build on an already-existing superego. Nevertheless, Freud did detect a providential, protective element in the superego. Despite his remark that 'The superego seems to have made a one-sided choice and to have picked out only the parents' strictness and severity, their prohibiting and punitive function, whereas their loving care seems not to have been taken over and maintained,'[14] he states elsewhere that 'The superego fulfils the same function of protecting and saving that was fulfilled in earlier days by the father.'[15] The discrepancy between these statements is probably to be explained as a consequence of the very thing we are discussing — the obscurity of the early, providential superego-precursors in the individual and their later submergence in the punitive, Oedipal superego, a complication which does not, of course, occur in the cultural evolution of the superego. Thus even though a clearly recognizable individual equivalent of the mother-godddesses of primal agriculture will probably never be found in early childhood, there is some reason to believe

[14] *New Introductory Lectures on Psychoanalysis*, XXII, p. 62.
[15] *The Ego and the Id*, XIX, p. 58.

that it may manifest itself later in life. We are certainly justifed in assuming that in the constitution of the super-ego, both love and need for, as well as hatred and fear of, the parents play a part. Furthermore, of the two opposite currents of feeling, the positive, needing one is probably the older and more fundamental.

If this is true, then it strongly suggests that things are indeed not as simple as they may have seemed. If a need for parental protection in part constitutes the superego — and a fundamental, primitive part at that — then it may be that disturbances in later superego-formation will bring these earlier, more primitive, aspects of the superego to the fore. We have already encountered an archetypal example of this in the Neolithic mother-goddess cult, and it may be that today, over-indulged children, not fully weaned because of permissive fashions in modern child-rearing, and encouraged throughout their childhood and adolescence to remain dependent on parents who have been afraid to deny them anything, experience a similar hankering after the unobtainable but mouth-watering mother-as-breast. And just as late Palaeolithic and early Neolithic cultures demonstrated their difficulty in detaching themselves from the primal mother of the previous epoch, so modern youth expresses its inability to surmount the oral attachment by coupling its parricidal protest against authority with a simultaneous and equally insistent demand for *welfare*. Indeed, as we have seen, such an infantile fixation at a pre-genital stage is an inevitable consequence of the very thing which explains the protests and the revolt against authority — the inability to transcend the phallic, Oedipal phase.

In an age of secularization, in which religious myths have been ruthlessly unmasked and in which parricidal revolt and protest has been directed as much against God as against other father-surrogates, it is not surprising that a regressive current of feeling, comparable to that which sustained the Neolithic goddess-cults, no longer finds an obvious religious expression. Nevertheless, in the light of these considerations it is hard to escape the impression that, like the Venus of Willendorf, or the many-breasted Diana of Ephesus, the modern welfare state has become the re-embodiment of the primal mother, the abstract, secular, bureaucratic equivalent of the mother-as-breast. Indeed, far from being merely analogous with the Neolithic situation, we have an exact historical recapitulation because, as we saw, the primal mother, lost on earth, phantasied in heaven, soon achieved a genuine reincarnation in the welfare state divine monarchies, where absolute monarchs tempered their tyranny with protection and sustenance of their citizens through their monopolization of the economic surplus and the means of coercive power. If authoritarian welfare states fulfilled these atavistic needs in the Neolithic, there is every reason to believe that they could still do so today; and certainly there is much evidence to show that modern police states, far from merely fulfilling some of the same psychological functions, even mimic their Neolithic forerunners in the details of their ritual and symbolism, and certainly seem to evolve their own thorough-going political religions.

Even the apparent differences turn out to be manifestations of the same latent wish for the protection and love of the parent. In the Neolithic period, totalitarian states emerged as a result of the reappearance of profound inequalities made possible by the acquisition of agricultural surpluses, whereas in the modern epoch most of the comparable states emerged out of periods of revolution and upheaval constituted mainly by a struggle for equality — a fact that has had the odd consequence of leaving all modern police states with official ideologies strongly committed to a non-existent freedom and egalitarianism for their citizens. Yet there can be little doubt that this demand for equality, even though not apparent in the Neolithic case, but so insistent and widespread in all modern societies, is a direct consequence of seeing the state as the milch-mother. If there are many siblings who must compete for the mother's favours, and if no one of them can exclude the others, each will probably demand equality as the next best thing to preference, and most definitely as the best way of preventing the preference of others. Envy, a well-known oral character trait which is at the root of this demand for equality, is one of the most prominent features of modern welfare state societies.

The way in which some modern political leaders exploit envy for their own purposes, and the way it is built into some party programmes, positively suggest that this is a powerful current of feeling which can be readily and effectively exploited. Even those who demand equality for others but nothing for themselves are not necessarily motivated by pure altruism and disinterestedness, as the following clinical example shows':

> An employee who would never venture to ask for a raise in salary for herself suddenly besieged the manageress with demands that one of her fellow workers should have her rights. Analysis of such situations shows that this defensive process has its origin in the infantile conflict with parental authority about some form of instinctual gratification. Aggressive impulses against the mother, prohibited as long as it is a question of fulfilling the subject's own wishes, are given rein when the wishes are ostensibly those of someone else. The most familiar representative of this type of person is the public benefactor, who with the utmost aggressiveness and energy demands money from one set of people in order to give it to another.[16]

Of course, the welfare state is the public benefactor magnified into an entire system of government.

[16] Anna Freud, *The Ego and the Mechanisms of Defence*, pp. 129–30.

The foregoing considerations will, I hope, have been enough to show that, from the psychological point of view, it is no paradox that the political and social revolutions of modern times which have opposed traditional (i.e., paternal) authorities and replaced them with more egalitarian (i.e., fraternal) structures have also brought into being a massively enhanced state apparatus to feed the appetite for welfare provisions. The fundamental psychological truth is that the parent – be it mother or father – is both loved *and* hated. Hence if one trend in modern culture corresponds to hatred of the parents and a desire to be rid of them and their authority, another equally insistent one demands their protection, their love, their provision of all that one cannot provide for oneself — in short, welfare. This is why modern governments, which must satisfy the demands for fraternal egalitarianism of the sons (and the daughters), must also satisfy their demands for paternalistic beneficence in the form of the modern welfare state. The state must, therefore, like the parents of early childhood, protect the citizen and satisfy all his needs; the state must, again like the parent of the infant, forgive, indulge and tolerate all his activities, even the parricidal, aggressive ones; it must accept all criticism, but never criticize in its turn; it must provide, but never demand in its turn; it must love, cherish and value, but accept hatred, indifference and contempt in return. It must in effect become the actual embodiment of the idealized, phantasied parent of early childhood, the parent who is omnipresently nurturing, omnisciently caring and omnipotently protecting. Only when this phantasy is well on the way to realization as a practical mode of government does the citizen begin to notice that the state's omnipresence means the total bureaucratization and control of life, that its omniscience dictates the need for total state surveillance, and that its omnipotence can only come about as a consequence of the total impotence of its subjects.

The fundamental reason for this is a fact of ego-psychology which the individualistic fallacy and the therapeutic tunnel-vision of modern psychotherapy obscures. It is simply that a permissive culture which makes increasingly fewer demands on the egos and superegos of its citizens where self-restraint, postponement of gratification and drive-inhibition in general are concerned must — unless it is to dissolve in anarchy — abrogate those restraining, controlling and inhibiting functions to itself and to its agencies of social control. Here, in the regressive, infantile wish for the perfect parent of early childhood lies the germ of the police state.

Something like this appears to have occurred in the great Near Eastern empires in the post-Neolithic period; and it certainly occurred in Inca Peru. We can now see clearly why it is that once great state dominations appear which have the means to minutely command and control the lives of their citizens, those citizens can relieve themselves of the discomfiting need to exercise personal self-restraint or economic forethought for the simple and adequate reason that the state now exercises these ungratifying functions for them. 'As for provident concern for the future,' in the case of the Peruvians of the Inca state,

> how could that have been developed among a people whose public granaries were crammed with provisions and whose public officials were authorized to distribute them in case of need? There was never any need to think beyond the necessities of the moment. 'The Indians today,' remarks Ondegardo, 'never think of getting a new garment until the old one is in tatters'. 'They take no thought for the morrow,' says Cabeza de Vaca . . . On the rare occasions when the Indian does seek to build up a reserve for himself, he squanders it at once.[17]

[17] L. Baudin, *A Socialist Empire: The Incas of Peru*, Princeton, 1961, pp. 201–2.

The Psychopathology of Present-day Life 111

This improvident and unself-disciplined behaviour was a direct consequence of the Inca welfare system in which 'a subsistence minimum was assured to every individual, absolute destitution was unknown, and great inequalities of fortune were and remained exceptional. A man could not become completely impoverished, but it only rarely happened that anyone grew rich.'[18] That the provision of egalitarian welfare was also implicitly a means of social control emerges clearly: 'The Peruvian government knew how to hold in check passions destructive of the social order and to prevent the revival of primitive anarchy. The Incas banished the two great causes of popular disaffection: *poverty* and *idleness*, and they left only a small place for ambition and greed.'[19] Indeed, as one account put it, 'The Incas ruled their people in such a way that there was among them neither a thief nor a vicious man nor a sluggard nor an adulterous woman . . .'[20]

In these great welfare state totalitarianisms therefore, as in the modern world, child-rearing regimes could regress to pre-agricultural styles, and oral indulgence, Oedipal rivalry and incestuous fixation could all be allowed to occur in the individual because the state bureaucracies would see to it that none of the undesirable consequences of these things occurred in reality. Now the state, instead of the individual, controlled consumption in the interests of conservation; the state exercised initiative and decision-making functions in place of those of the individual's ego; and the state institutions of social control enforced law and order in the place of the superego. Hence the growth of state power meant the enslavement of individuals who became totally dependent on it for everything and who, as individuals, no longer possessed the personal responsibil-

---

[18] *Ibid.*, p. 198.
[19] *Ibid.*, p. 200.
[20] *Ibid.*, p. 40.

ity for any but the most trivial and harmless of their actions:

> The Indian did not have to do any thinking for himself. The government thought and acted for him, and if its action was suspended, social life would stop short. Under the rule of the Incas this inertia expressed itself in the stagnation of commerce . . . in the lack of vitality and the absence of originality in the arts, in dogmatism in science, and in the rareness of even the simplest inventions.[21]

All this was a direct and ineluctable consequence of the fact that the ego which fails to mature and master its drives must either be mastered by them or have them mastered on its behalf by some external force. If the former cannot be allowed to happen because this spells an end to society, then external coercion must come to replace internal restraint; and drives which cannot be inhibited and redirected by the ego and superego must instead be mastered by agencies of social control. If we try to describe this process in structural terms we will have to say that this externalization of forces of control leads to a marked deterioration and dissolution of the superego and, to a lesser extent, of the ego too.

Earlier on I quoted Freud's remarks to the effect that in the course of human development 'external coercion gradually becomes internalized' and that this internalization produces the superego.[22] Freud refers to this process of strengthening of the superego as the 'most precious cultural asset', and observes that it turns enemies of civilization into its vehicles, and greatly enhances the security of culture. But the line of cultural development represented by Inca Peru and increasingly by modern welfare states runs quite counter to this. In the latter case external coer-

---

[21] *Ibid.*, pp. 200–1.
[22] See above, p. 68 and Freud, XXI, p. 11.

cion is no longer internalized in the way it once was because of the permissive regimes of child-rearing and a cultural crisis affecting the superego, about which more will be said later. In these societies it cannot be accidental that as revolt and protest against traditional values and restraints have grown, so too have the means of external coercion represented by police forces, government agencies, legislation, taxation and a generalized bureaucratic regulation of just about every important aspect of the citizen's life. Certainly, we are surrounded by unmistakable signs of the decreasing security of our culture and the fact that more and more of its erstwhile vehicles are becoming its enemies.

In the Inca state this process of regression seems not merely to have profoundly compromised the superego and to have replaced it with the person of the Inca and his fellow Children of the Sun, but also to have attacked the ego in general and to have reduced the Indians to an apathetic, dependent and passive state in which the higher ego-functions of decision-making, initiative, and individuality were markedly reduced. This regression of the superego and degradation of the ego was readily noticed by Spanish visitors to the Inca empire who commented on the lack of personality development and the general childlikeness of the Indians:

> In most of the provinces . . . the natives used to copy one another so effectively that they could be looked upon as all identical . . . . The Indians, like children, differed from one another more in external appearance than by virtue of distinctive personal qualities. Everything was alike; men resembled each other as if they were all brothers. In every isolated basin of the plateau the life led by the common people day after day was as monotonous as the climate and the landscape; and everything that deviated from the ordinary, everything strange or unforeseen, was regarded

as supernatural. This is the final result toward which all the great socialist reformers have tended . . .[23]

'If,' says Baudin in conclusion, 'it is the development of the personality that is regarded as the goal of human existence, then the Peruvian system was the most disastrous of all social experiments. The Inca plunged his subjects into a sleep akin to death. He robbed them of all dignity.'[24]

The loss of dignity, indivduality, initiative, decisiveness and independence which nearly all the observers report of the Peruvians is the consequence of ego-degradation and replacement of the superego by the external coercion of the state. The resulting drab uniformity and melancholy of mood which struck Spanish visitors to the Inca empire no less than the lack of personality of its inhabitants provides an interesting and instructive parallel with socialist socieities of today. But the phenomenon of mild chronic depression in total states is probably not unrelated to parallel depressive tendencies to which I have already alluded when discussing the manic-depressive morphology of primal agriculture.

We saw earlier that the loss of the all-provident mother of the hunter-gatherer economy with the coming of agriculture and its childhood corollary, traumatic weaning, resulted in a depressive tendency brought about, as in modern clinical depression, through identification with an introjected, lost object and its subsequent punishment within the self. In the totalitarian state however, agriculture does not have quite the same result. We have already seen why it is that traumatic weaning may no longer be necessary because the state, rather than the individual's own ego and superego, now enforces postponement of

---

[23] Baudin, *A Socialist Empire: the Incas of Peru*, p. 203.
[24] *Ibid.*, p. 207.

oral gratification in the interest of the economy. But for all this, the fact remains that the citizen of the agricultural welfare state is not a primal hunter-gatherer. He may indeed be relatively unweaned and improvident like his hunter-gatherer forefathers, but the reality is that he lives in a highly regulated agricultural economy in which the largely uninhibited oral and anal-sadistic drives of the hunter-gatherer are subject to strict state-control. The result of this, as far as the individual is concerned, is still inevitably depression and its polar opposite mania, except that in these circumstances depression has become the vague permanent melancholy which state oppression invariably induces, and the intermittent mania is that produced by alcohol.

As to the melancholy or chronic mild depression which socialist totalitarianisms seem to induce, it is obvious that individuals who have not mastered oral, anal and phallic instinctual drives within their own personalities cannot derive the gain in self-esteem, self-control and narcissistic self-satisfaction which the successful surmounting of an instinctual conflict always brings. Such mastery of basic drives may cost the ego something, but it also brings rich rewards. By learning to control its basic instinctual drives, the ego establishes its mastery over them and is freed from its enslavement to them. While the unweaned child must remain preoccupied by the absence of the breast and his hunger for it, the successfully weaned individual is free to turn his attention to other means of satisfying his hunter, and will probably find that, as in the instructive case of agriculture, a judicious control of his appetite results in the long run in a lessened likelihood of hunger. The orally fixated individual however, like the primal hunter-gatherer, cannot achieve such a self-mastery and must rely on his luck to feed whenever and wherever he may need to do so. (Even today, Australian aborigines who have lived for a generation in settlements have still to acquire the habit of taking regular meals.[25]) The latter attitude is compatible with an irregular, insecure food resource like game, but is quite incompatible with the requirements of the rational use of food resources found in agriculture.

The practical consequence of this must be that the individual who in his personal development has not mastered his basic instinctual drives but finds instead that the state masters them for him experiences none of the narcissistic gratifications of self-mastery but all of the privations which the agencies of state control enforce on him. Thus whereas mastery of the instinctual drives builds the ego and raises its level of self-esteem and competence, its individuality and its initiative, external control of those drives has the opposite effect, reducing the self-esteem, competence, initiative and individuality of the ego to the point where it almost disappears altogether. This external punishment of, and reduction in, the ego exactly parallels the internal punitive and self-depreciating tendencies found in clinical depression and, to a much lesser extent, in normal mourning. It is almost as if what the ego is subjected to by the superego in clinical depression is what the state does to the individual in totalitarian states, namely, it punishes the self with renunciation of instinctual drives, with reduced self-esteem and with a curtailment of its competence and freedom of activity.

Another important symptom of clinical depression is loss of the capacity to love.[26] This results from the preoccupation of the ego with its lost object and its inability to detach its libido from it. An analogous situation is reported in the case of the Inca state:

> the substitution of the state for the individual in the econ-

---

[25] Personal communication from Dr David McKnight.
[26] Freud, 'Mourning and Melancholia', XIV, p. 244.

omic domain destroyed the *spirit of charity*. The native Peruvian, expecting the state to do everything, no longer had to concern himself with his fellow man and had to come to his aid only if required by law . . . They had to help their neighbors if ordered to do so by their chiefs, but they were obliged to to nothing on their own initiative. That is why, by the time of the Spanish conquest, the most elementary humanitarian feelings were in danger of disappearing entirely.[27]

If the reader is tempted to doubt the general validity of such a concrete and specific historical instance, let me remind him that Campanella — an ostensibly Christian author, be it noted — makes it perfectly clear that in his socialist utopia, the City of the Sun, 'no one can receive gifts from another. Whatever is necessary they have, they receive it from the community, and the magistrate takes care that no one receives more than he deserves.'[28] Clearly, then, the loss of an individual's concern for the welfare of his fellows is a matter of principle in these circumstances, not historical accident.

As in the previous instances, this loss of the capacity to love does not originate in a process within the ego as it does in clinical depression but, in the case of the welfare state totalitarianisms, in an externalization of comparable phenomena. However, one factor — and that, perhaps the most important — in both clinical depression and welfare totalitarianism is fundamentally identical. It is what Freud called in a memorable phrase, *an impoverishment of the ego on a grand scale.*[29] It is precisely this which is lacking in normal mourning, which is otherwise the closest approximation to clinical depression, and, as we can now

---

[27] Baudin, *A Socialist Empire: the Incas of Peru,* p. 202.
[28] Campanella, 'The City of the Sun', in H. Morley (ed.), *Ideal Commonwealths,* London, 1885, p. 226.
[29] 'Mourning and Melancholia', XIV, p. 246.

see, constitutes the central pathological process both in the latter and in its collective, externalized equivalent, the melancholy of socialism:

> Among no other peoples in the New World do we find, as we do in the realm of the Incas, a slow and gradual absorption of the individual by the state. The poison was not given to the Indians in massive doses that would have provoked a reaction, but was administered drop by drop, until it brought about the loss of personality. Man was made for the state, and not the state for the man. This is indeed socialism in the full sense of the word . . . . The Indian had nothing to do but obey; and whoever has formed the habit of passive obedience ends by being no longer able to act for himself and comes to love the yoke that is laid upon him. Nothing is easier than to obey a master who is perhaps exacting, but who rules over all details of life, assures one's daily bread, and makes it possible to banish all concern from the mind.[30]

If clinical depression represents improvishment of the ego on a grand scale, then here we have it on a scale which can only be called grander still: that of an entire culture, a complete philosophy of life.

Turning now to the manic alternative to depression, we find that in welfare totalitarianisms periodic alcoholic intoxication constitutes the externalized equivalent of the purely psychic state of intoxication which is produced by internal means in the manic individual. The reason for this is easily appreciated; it originates in the widely known fact that the superego (and, to a lesser extent the ego) possesses the notable psychological property of being — figuratively speaking — partly soluble in alchohol! Indeed, in his discussion of mania in 'Mourning and Melancholia' Freud remarks that 'Alcoholic intoxication . . . belongs to the

---

[30] Baudin, *A Socialist Empire: the Incas of Peru*, pp. 199–200.

same class of states.'[31] Furthermore, in his continued discussion of the problem in *Group Psychology and the Analysis of the Ego* he likens the manic state to festivals such as the Roman Saturnalia, 'which owe their cheerful character to the release which they bring'.[32]

At first sight it may seem surprising that if, as I am claiming, the superego is underdeveloped in welfare totalitarianisms because the means of state coercion are overdeveloped, it should nevertheless need to be dissolved in anything. After all, in the discussions to which I have just referred, Freud maintains that essential to the manic state is a temporary fusion between the ego and the superego and a resulting reduction in tension which allows a joyful release of the energies previously bound up in their antagonism. However, we must not forget that even in a welfare totalitarianism like Inca Peru the individual still has some sort of rudimentary superego, albeit perhaps only the primitive one of early childhood; and, furthermore, we must not overlook his explanation of the feeling of triumph present in mania. This originates, he says, 'when something in the ego coincides with the ego ideal'[33] (or superego). Now, as we have already seen, the externalization of coercion and the failure of the ego to come to terms with its basic instinctual drives in the total state robs it of nearly all its opportunity to experience such triumphs. In these circumstances the ego simply has no hope of triumphing by measuring up to the ideal standards of the superego, in so far as it exists. Therefore the only satisfaction which the ego can obtain in this way is to lower the tension between itself and whatever superego it has until it brings the ideal down to its own level, rather than aspiring to reach it. Indeed, if the superego is always

---

[31] XIV, p. 254.
[32] XVIII, p. 131.
[33] *Ibid.*

in part a cultural, collective phenomenon and if in such states the divine monarch, chairman or party leader is far beyond the reach of the identifications of the masses because of his incomparable pre-eminence, then it follows that only in the dissolution of the superego that alcohol brings does the ordinary ego find any hope of believing, however unrealistically, that it is equal to, or as worthy as, the father of the state. In short, if the ego cannot aspire to the ideal, alcoholic intoxication may bring the ideal down to the ego. Certainly, its capacity to dull the sense of reality must be very welcome in societies in which the chastizement of the superego is externalized as an oppressive and very real coercive force. Thus it is possible that the chronic alcoholism reported in some socialist utopias in the East may have the same psychological roots as that so vividly described by the Spanish chroniclers of Inca Peru.

Finally, it is worth pointing out that, if my account of neoteny in man is correct, even the relatively ego-less citizen of the totalitarian state is the possessor of what we might term the neurophysiological substrate of the ego and the superego, which almost certainly comprises some of the most recently acquired elements of the human brain. Perhaps only a state of intoxication brought about by suppressants of these centres can really suffice to effect the final dissolution of the superego which, being after all a purely psychological agency, cannot literally be soluble in alcohol.

If we contrast this collective alcoholic mania with the manic structure which I have attributed to the personality of the ruler of such totalitarian societies we can see an intersting opposition. In the case which we have just been discussing, that of the common, oppressed people, it is a question of the superego being degraded by alcoholic intoxication to the point where it and the ego can merge (or, at least where it no longer chastizes the ego); but in the case of the Inca himself we saw that it was a case of a pre-eminent individual whose ego was exalted to the point where it became the ideal ego of the entire civilization. The latter condition seems much closer to megalomania, which we understand to be an immense inflation of the ego, whereas the former seems more like the manic interludes in depression. However, what both share is the merging, whether temporary as in the case of the intoxication, or permanent in the case of the monarch, of the ego and superego and the resulting release from the oppression of the latter. But the distinction between these two kinds of mania is probably fundamental, and it is noteworthy that its social equivalents should closely model its individual manifestations. Thus megalomania in individual madness is usually a much more permanent state than the mania of manic-depression; and in the former case there is no doubt that the ego has undergone a vast elevation in its own estimation. Whether we would be correct to conclude from this that in manic-depression mania was produced by a quasi-toxic suppression of the superego I do not know, but if would certainly accord well with Freud's suggestion that in the manic interludes in depression we witness 'a magnificent festival of the ego, which might then once again feel satisfied with itself'.[34]

Expressed in developmental, rather than structural terms, one can describe the condition of the citizens of total welfare states as childlike, for not only are they likely to be regressed in developmental terms for the reasons already given, they are also childlike in relative terms to the state which has become a parent, and an omnipotent one at that. Indeed, even in the as yet relatively non-totalitarian welfare states of the West some have already discerned the

[34] *Group Psychology and the Analysis of the Ego*, XVIII, p. 131.

same paternalistic and enslaving trend: 'government's role is to serve as a parent charged with the duty of coercing some to aid others,' while government-funded welfare programmes 'put some people in a position to decide what is good for other people. The effect is to instil in one group a feeling of almost God-like power; in the other, a feeling of child-like dependence.'[35] We saw earlier that such a relationship of passive dependency on a parental power perceived as esssentially paternal might account for the undoubted paranoid elements which emerge along with the megalomania of the divine monarchs — itself the paranoid equivalent of depressive mania. It is probably not accidental that the most famous and widely discussed paranoiac of modern psychiatric literature, Schreber, had a father who seems to have approximated rather closely to the divine monarchs of earlier times and certainly practised a regime of child-rearing which was notable not only for its authoritarianism but also for its central concern for the welfare of the child, who was to be protected from harmful influences, bad habits and incorrect posture by rigidly enforced and total parental control, which even included applying iron and leather braces and restraints to the child's body. Schreber's father, who ruled his household like a dictator and believed that he had a mission to reform educational principles, acquired a large following, especially in Germany, and was compared favourably by one of his biographers with Hitler. According to Schreber *père's* theories,

> From the earliest age all strivings for independence, nonobedience to rules, passions and bad habits [read: masturbation] must be dealt with promptly and drastically. The means recommended here are verbal admonishments, mechanical restraint, and bodily punishment. A state of complete submissiveness can thus be established in

[35] M. and R. Friedman, *Free to Choose*, Harmondsworth, 1980, p. 149.

all children before they reach the fifth or sixth year of life . . .[36]

Here we have something that looks very much like a totalitarian welfare state in microcosm, and which must have powerfully contributed to Schreber's psychosis, which featured delusions of passive submission to impregnation by an omnipotent solar god. Such delusions are, as I pointed out earlier, typical of paranoia and are *projections*. Now we can begin to see that an externalization of the superego like that which occurs in total welfare states is closely allied to the projection of the superego met with in paranoia.

It is an arresting paradox — although, admittedly, only a seeming one — that where child-rearing veers to the exact opposite extreme to that represented by the Schreber case and becomes a liberal democracy, or even anarchy in microcosm, the eventual consequence, if I am correct, may well be a totalitarian macrocosm. Of course, the apparent paradox vanishes once we realize that in advanced industrial economies superego controls on behaviour may not be optional if public order, production and economic surpluses are to be defended, and that if these controls cannot be procured internally they will be externalized in the organs of the police state. Yet, as we have already seen, even in a situation like this, primitive internal superego structures are still likely to exist, even if these are not mature enough to render external coercion unnecessary. It is these residual, archaic superego elements which combine with the more rational, mature ones in the comprehensive externalization of the superego which occurs in total societies. For we have already seen that there is no reason why, along with the mature elements of

---

[36] W. G. Niederland, 'Schreber's Father', *Journal of the American Psychoanalytic Association*, 8 (1960), p. 496.

the superego which serve the interests of adjustment to reality, immature, primitive elements should not also become externalized in those aspects of the state which represent it as nurturing, protecting and providing some measure of wish fulfilment for the most regressive desires. Yet it is these very passive, dependent wishes for the omnipotent, omniscient and omnipresent parent which seem to give rise to the conflicts which are central to paranoia. They are also the very wishes which in total welfare states lead to what we may justly term the externalization of paranoia: for in these totalitarian societies the delusions of the paranoiac become actual, tangible realities. The state does become omnipotent and now the delusion of passive impotence — perhaps the central conflict in paranoia — becomes a reality. From the regressive, infantile phantasy of the omniscient parent comes the very common paranoid delusion of always being watched which, in the totalitarian state, achieves an all too real fulfilment in the extensive surveillance to which all its citizens are subjected. Here, delusions of persecution become actualized if, as not unusually happens, the interests of the the citizen come into conflict with those of a state which has monopolized all the means of coercive power. It is a common complaint of institutionalized paranoiacs in the West that they are perfectly sane and being persecuted by psychiatrists; in certain socialist utopias in the East it is sometimes the literal truth. But this is not some chance paradox of history; it arises in the psychological truth that in modern totalitarian states the purely internal and irrational conflicts of the psychoses can become external and quite real.

'Perhaps,' I can hear my readers saying, 'but you cannot possibly suppose that all the totalitarian states which have come into existence in times ancient and modern have been the result of faulty socialization and nothing more.' They will probably correctly object that this theory of mine seems to get things round the wrong way, and that even if we grant my argument that growth in the power of the state detracts from that of the individual's superego, there is every reason to suppose that in most cases the total power came first, and the deterioration in personality, however we like to describe it, later. Of course, this a justified objection; and I am ready to concede that in most historical examples one might like to point out things probably did happen that way round. But, let me say by way of rejoinder, there is no necessary reason why things should not come about the other way round — with the personality regression preceding the growth in power of the state — and that even if this is a functional, rather than causal, relationship, it is nevertheless a significant one. Furthermore, I think that my readers will readily grant that in reality these two phenomena usually go hand-in-hand to create a vicious and self-sustaining circle of growth in state power promoting individual impotence causing more state power, etc. Finally, it is worth pointing out that in some modern societies there is considerable reason to suppose that, as yet, the ego and superego-degradation has gone a lot further then the externalization of the superego functions of the state, but that there is no reason why in these circumstances the externalization process should not rapidly catch up. State institutions, we should remember, can change a good deal faster than child-rearing regimes or basic personality types.

One further, historical point will not be out of place. If we restrict our attention solely to the twentieth century, it is notable that the two most important and traumatic socialist revolutions, that in Russia in 1917 and that in Germany during the Nazi era, whilst being the creation of particular political leaders who soon imposed total state power, nevertheless drew what popular support they had from political myths that are obvious paranoid projections. In the case of both international Marxist socialism and German National Socialism, the centre-piece of the party programme was the liberation of the masses from exploitation and persecution by money-makers, Jews in the one case, capitalists in the other (of course, as I have shown elsewhere,[37] the latter is derived from the former and the former is only a somewhat secularized version of traditional Christian anti-Semitism). In the unconscious, money and gold are universally understood to be symbols of faeces,[38] and it cannot be accidental that analysis of individual delusions of persecution shows that the persecuting object is usually the child's phantasied idea of the paternal phallus as the retained and hardened faecal mass in its bowel.[39] In both individual, internalized, and in collective, externalized, paranoid delusions, the common feature of projection employs this regressive, anal phantasy because the anus is the nearest male equivalent to the receptive, passive, enclosing vagina of the female. If in both cases passive surrender to an ominpotent phantasied father-figure is the centre of the conflict, then it is intelligible that this should be projected as the infantile equivalent of castrating, homosexual, anal rape. Thus what the power, wealth, cunning and conspiratiorial danger of the Jews really stand for in National Socialism, or what the capitalists represent in International Socialism, is the annihilating phantasy-phallus of the omnipotent father of the earliest and most primitive superego. In this way projections, which are partial externalizations, paved the way for the full-scale externalization of paranoia which afflicted

---

[37] *The Psychoanalysis of Culture*, pp. 233–9.

[38] *The Psychoanalysis of Culture*, p. 200; also E. Borneman (ed.), *The Psychoanalysis of Money*, New York, 1976.

[39] A. Starcke, 'Reversal of the libido-sign in delusions of persecution'; and J. Van Ophuijsen, 'On the origin of the feeling of persecution', *International Journal of Psychoanalysis*, I (1929), pp. 231–9; J. Arlow, 'Anal sensations and feelings of persecution', *Psychoanalytic Quarterly*, 18 (1949) pp. 79–84; L. Bender, 'The anal component in persecutory delusions', *Psychoanalytic Review*, 21 (1934), pp. 75–85.

Germany under the Third Reich and which continues to afflict many Marxist states today. Finally, if my readers still have doubts about the general drift of my argument, let me ask them how else we are to explain why modern revolutionary movements which always aim to free those who believe in them always end by enslaving them? May it not be that the outcome reflects the real motive — the wish to procure an external realization of a regressive, inner phantasy, that of the supreme parent of earliest childhood? We should recall that man did not originally evolve in a liberal democracy, but in the primal horde.

If we now return to the basic theory of the ego, we can follow Freud[40] in seeing it as subject to three often conflicting demands: that of the instinctual drives of the id, that of the values of the superego, and that of reality. Should the ego fail to satisfy the id it becomes prey to neurotic anxiety arising out of the strength of its instinctual drives; if it fails the superego it is subject to moral anxiety; and if it cannot meet the demands of the outside world it is likely to experience realistic anxiety. If serious conflict breaks out with regard to any one of these types of demand the result will be either a neurosis (conflict between the ego and the id), a manic-depressive disorder (conflict between the ego and the superego), or a psychosis (conflict between the ego and reality).[41]

Yet our present line of argument shows that there is another possibility that, because of failures in individual and superego development, such conflicts will no longer be confined within the personality, but may break out between it and the outside world. The result is the phenomenon of externalization which we have been

---

[40] *New Introductory Lectures on Psychoanalysis*, XXII, pp. 77–8.
[41] Freud, 'Neurosis and psychosis', XIX, p. 152.

discussing. If we wish to know why hysteria is now so rare and why modern forms of psychopathology in general seem so often removed from their classical, nineteenth and early twentieth-century manifestations, we may now be in a position to give at least part of the answer. It is simply that these conflicts, which once would have been more or less wholly contained within the personality, are now becoming externalized and, indeed, are transforming society. Thus what would once have been typical neurotic conflicts between the ego and the id are much more likely to present themselves today as delinquency and compulsive acting-out. Now, conflicts between instinctual drives and the controlling agency occur more and more as social and political conflicts, and less and less as purely psychological ones. This is because the ego remains weak and ineffectual in the face of powerful instinctual demands owing to the inadequacy of the superego and the lack of cultural support.

Rather than attempting to stifle mental conflict and to keep it from consciousness as would have been the trend in nineteenth and early twentieth-century culture, modern cultural trends instead encourage acting-out and expression of the conflict as being more 'healthy' than repression. Yet the acting-out of conflict is no more healthy in a true sense than its repression if this externalization of it is compulsive and without insight. As in the case of the classical neurosis, the ego remains weak and ineffectual where the issues of the conflict are concerned and is just as much at its mercy. Indeed, the situation might actually be worse than the classical neurosis because at least in that case the chief symptoms of the disorder, for instance, neurotic anxiety, present themselves as definite psychopathic factors, whereas in an externalized, acted-out neurosis the symptoms may be reality factors that arise because of maladaptive behaviour which may mask its irrational, compulsive nature. For instance, someone who acts out neurotic conflicts by committing crimes like theft or robbery may be able to represent these activities even to himself as a response to material need rather than unconscious compulsion. The situation is compounded when such behaviour is 'explained' by some of the completely non-psychological — indeed, even militantly anti-psychological — theories of crime and delinquency which are fashionable today with sociologists, social workers and the general public. The fact is that an externalized conflict with a psychopathic origin can be confused all too easily with a genuinely external one.

Of course, we have a very good precedent for believing that internal, neurotic conflicts between the ego and the id can become externalized. This lies in the consideration that, in the beginning, they were externalized as the social conflict between the sons and the primal father. Internalization only followed as a consequence of that external conflict once the sons began to internalize the primal father through chronically ambivalent, guilt-ridden mourning for him. Thereafter, the entire conflict became internalized as the collective anxiety hysteria which we know today as totemic religion.

But what has become internalized can always become externalized again; and so we have seen that, increasingly in modern societies, anti-social instinctual drives of the id — specifically, the instinctual drives of the gelada-like sons of the primal fathers — break out in social conflicts and acts of delinquency and provocation which the modern incarnation of the primal father — the police, the Establishment, law, order and standards of all kinds — have to meet. In short, it is not that classical neuroses no longer exist, or that psychopathology has fundamentally changed — how could it? — but that such neuroses are perhaps increasingly acted-out and externalized as interpersonal conflicts rather than intrapsychic ones. In this respect the incidence of neurosis seems inversely proportional to social disorder. Neurotic anxiety is probably progressively giving way to social discontent, and as the centre of the conflict moves away from the ego into the society as a whole individual psychotherapy of whatever kind probably becomes increasingly difficult. Far from awaiting us in some dazzling future, as some might hope, the golden age of individual psychoanalytic therapy is probably already behind us. (However, throughout this discussion I have ignored those psychosomatic disorders which might be the consequence of what we could call 'somatic externalization'. I have no way of knowing how important a factor this is, but I suspect that it may be a vital one.)

In the absence of other, countervailing forces, this externalization of Oedipal conflict would seriously threaten the whole psychological basis of culture; it would threaten to undo all that millennia of civilization had achieved and would plunge humanity back into the savagery from which it had originally so painfully emerged. But, as we have seen, there are good reasons for thinking that such countervailing forces do indeed exist, principally in the archaic superego structures which, thanks to neoteny and the neurophysiological changes of the latency period, have become natural to man. These cortical consequences of social evolution provide the basis for the acquisition of some sort of superego, even if they cannot ensure that it is a rational, mature and adaptive one.

If we now turn our attention to the second type of conflict enumerated by Freud, that between the ego and the superego, we have already noticed that the externalization of the superego, particularly of its archaic and providential aspects, is easily possible and seemingly well under way in many societies. However, this reincarnation of the primitive providential parental images in the institutions of the modern state should not blind us to what is one of the most distressing and presently most serious effects of the externalization of what is fundamentally manic-depressive psychopathology.

In discussing the externalization of id/ego conflicts we saw that this effectively meant social and psychological regression to the situation immediately preceding the internalization of the conflict — in that case, to the conflicts of the primal horde. In earlier chapters we saw that manic-depressive conflict between ego and superego became much more marked with the introduction of agriculture and weaning, leading to the internalization of the primal, providential mother in phantasy because of her disappearance in reality, as symbolized, for instance, in the mother-goddess cult. Clearly, then, externalization of this process may in part result in an undoing and reversal of that internalization of dependency on the lost, providential mother. Yet the primal mother is no longer with us, least of all in modern industrial societies where regimes of child-rearing, although perhaps permissive, cannot provide for total maternal-dependency throughout life. On the contrary, recent cultural trends have encouraged masculinity and achievement outside the home in women, notwithstanding the vogue for permissiveness (of which in reality it is a part). Consequently, this fixation on the earliest, nurturing and nutritive superego-precursor seems increasingly to express itself in the form of drug-addiction.

In his discussion of the problem, Otto Fenichel mentions 'food addicts' who 'are compelled violently and compulsively to devour whatever food is in reach at the moment.'[42] We can see that, in these terms, all immediate-return hunter-gatherers qualify as 'food addicts' because, never having been weaned, they retain the primal, nutritive addiction to the breast. Yet for them, such a personality-type is compatible with their way of life, and even beneficial (certainly, they never seem to suffer from the obesity that afflicts food addicts in societies with storable food-surpluses). An externalization — or, perhaps we should more strictly say, a *de-internalization* — or

---

[42] *The Psychoanalytic Theory of Neurosis*, p. 376.

dependency on the breast produces some external dependency which, if it does not manifest itself with regard to food, is likely to do so in an even more undesirable way with regard to addictive drugs or alcohol.

The appeal of drugs or alcohol probably lies in their ability to induce a state of transient mania which serves as a defence against the fundamental depression which dependency-through-loss brings about.[43] Admittedly, drugs and alcohol produce their own depressive 'morning-after' nemesis, but, as we have already seen, such reality-effects probably mask internal realities which the externalization of the conflict serves to obscure. While not doubting the pharmacological dimension to drug-addiction, it is nevertheless true to say that in many cases this is only an external consequence of an existing internal dependency which is just as addictive, even though repressed.

We have already noted a connection between intermittent alcoholic mania and the growth of state power, and so it seems that these two apparently unrelated phenomena are in reality both part of the same process. Whereas one is the externalization of the phantasied superego, the other is the externalization of dependency on, and defence against, it. The defensive aspect does not stand in any sort of opposition to the externalized one because of course externalization is a defensive process. It aims to save the ego from anxiety and conflict by removing the causes from the inner to the outer world. As such, it is a primitive defence mechanism often encountered in young children[44] and, as we have seen, is the basis of projection, a self-evidently defensive measure. Nevertheless, we should perhaps ask, 'Defensive for whom?' Obviously, the

---

[43] *Ibid.*, p. 378, quoting E. Simmel (1930).

[44] Anna Freud, *Normality and Pathology in Childhood*, London, 1966, p. 35.

answer is, 'For the ego,' but we have no right to suppose that it is equally defensive for the culture. Here, anything that threatens the superego tends to be destructive; and we can readily see that the externalization of conflict, although defensive for the ego, may be damaging for the culture because the effect of the externalization is to make the culture the locus of the conflict.

The third and last of Freud's categories of basic psychopathology, the psychotic conflict between the ego and reality, seems an unpromising candidate for externalization; and perhaps this is why the incidence of psychosis shows no sign of diminishing in modern culture in the way in which, for instance, hysteria has diminished. The reason that it seems unpromising follows directly from the Freudian theory of psychosis which sees it essentially as a withdrawal of libido from objects and its reinvestment in the ego. One can either see externalization as undoing this process and therefore no longer serving the ego in its defensive purpose, or one can see the psychotic remodelling of reality which occurs, for instance, in hallucination, as an all-too-successful externalization.

Nevertheless, we have already seen that it is possible to see some total societies as externalizations of paranoia; not merely as collective projections (which may also be present), but as realizations of paranoid processes within the architecture of the state. True schizophrenias, on the other hand, may not be possible to externalize in the same way because they lack the superego elements present in paranoia and because they represent much more radical breaks with reality.

However, looked at from another point of view, all externalizations of psychological conflict, be they morphologically neurotic, manic-depressive or psychotic, bring the ego into a disturbed, conflict-ridden relation to reality which renders all externalized psychopathology psychotic to that extent. It may be that bizarre, self-destructive and anti-social behaviour which would once only have afflicted the true psychotic will increasingly come to typify what would otherwise have been purely neurotic disorders had they been internalized as hitherto. This would imply that not only is psychopathology becoming increasingly externalized, but also increasingly schizoid in appearance. Indeed, if we go so far as to see externalization as inevitably bringing the ego into conflict with reality, then we might conclude that many modern neuroses — perhaps the most severe ones — are likely to become *para-psychoses*: that is, neurotic conflicts expressing themselves in the language of psychosis.

6
Art, Externalization and Insight

In our survey of the phenomenon of externalization in modern culture there has so far been one rather notable exception. This is the case of art and literature. My failure to mention it up to this point might be explained as a consequence of the fact that art, after all, is not unique to the modern world. On the contrary, it is a traditional form of externalization of fantasy and feeling which is found, in one form or another, in all cultures. However, perhaps because of this, modern art and literature emerge as the one great exception to the point which was made at the conclusion of the last chapter. Here we find an externalization of psychological states which is unmistakably schizoid and which bears all the signs of a psychotic conflict with, and flight from, reality.

It seems a coincidence too great to put down to chance that in the case of painting the first school of 'modernism' — impressionism — emerged within two decades of the taking of the first real photographs by Fox Talbot in 1841. Indeed, I would go further and say that nearly all of so-called 'modern' painting can be cogently and elegantly explained by one simple hypothesis: namely, that those styles of modern art which have acquired the labels 'modernist', 'avant-garde', etc., are all, in their revealingly different ways, reactions to the trauma represented by the invention and widespread use of the photographic camera.

The nature of the trauma is easy to grasp. Up until the coming of photography the pictorial artist knew exactly what he was supposed to do and knew increasingly well how to do it. His function was to depict reality and to describe it in an aesthetically pleasing fashion, whether it was a portrait, landscape, *genre* scene, or whatever. Yet the moment the photograph appeared some (although admittedly not all) artists became, effectively, enemies of modern culture and of the technology which, in the form of the camera, threatened to undermine the artistic *raison d'être*.

At the beginning, their reaction was a moderate and understandable one. In effect they said, 'Well, if the photograph can reproduce reality better in many ways than we can, let us compete by reproducing those aspects of reality which the camera cannot capture. Let us capture the effects of light.' At this time, the 1860s and 1870s, the colour photograph had of course not been developed to any great extent and no camera could reproduce the grainy, textured rendering of light effects in which the Impressionists so much delighted. The moment the first true colour photographs became available soon after 1900, the 'modern' artist, finding that photography could become as 'Impressionistic' as a painting, turned to other, more extreme measures. Indeed, almost from the beginnings of Impressionism, paintings began to look increasingly unfinished, with brush-marks and what in former days would have been called under-painting left clearly revealed. Indeed, some artists, such as Cézanne, for instance, seem to have done nothing but such schematic under-painting and to have begun the trend towards increasing abstraction and schematization which in time produced Cubism, Fauvism and Abstractionism. If the paint-work, brush-marks and so on were now so obvious, there was no danger of confusion with photographs as there had been in earlier days when realism and a highly polished finish made pictures look uncomfortably like colour photographs.

Now the artist began to give up all pretence at representation. First, as we have seen, he competed with the camera by concentrating on the effects of light; then, in the early years of this century when light too fell victim to the colour photograph, he turned to Cubism and to perspective effects which could never be achieved by a simple photograph, or to Fauvism, whose starkly simplified renderings and unreal colours were unmistakably 'artistic'. Then, when this position too fell to photo-montage and other photographic techniques, artists retreated either into pure abstraction, which, unlike the photograph, did not attempt to represent anything, or into Expressionism, a movement in which the gesture of painting became all-important (and which combined with the former trend in abstract expressionism). Finally, in more recent times, but beginning with Marcel Duchamp in the earlier part of this century, another defence was found. When Duchamp upturned a urinal, signed it (pseudonymously, though) and sent it to an art exhibition as a 'fountain' he was in effect saying that the only difference between the work of art and the everyday object was that an artist had decided that it was 'artistic' (and also very obviously an equivalent of exhibiting his genital, in itself a nice example of the regressive, infantile nature of much so-called 'art'). This led to the final closure of the circle in which artists denied the conflict with realistic, photographic representation by beginning to use real objects or photographic images and claiming to make them 'art' by changing their colour, exhibiting them in unusual contexts, or just by signing them. In the meantime abstract art, not seeking to represent anything, had succeeded in representing absolutely nothing, as in Malevitch's *White Square on White Background*, or the English artist who recently exhibited thirty-nine identical plain white canvases. In an ultimate attempt to become totally arbitrary and safe from confusion with photography artists have encouraged spectators to draw their pictures for them or have exhibited 'concept art' — pictures which only exist in the mind of the beholder.

It seems, in short, that modern painting has been dominated by a flight from reality occasioned by the traumatic irruption of photography into an otherwise traditional and secure field of art. It is thus no coincidence that modern art has come increasingly to resemble the art-work of psychotics and children — regressive forms of expression in which the image undergoes disintegration, schematization and degradation just as it does in the history of modern painting. The qualitative changes seen in the art-work of artistically talented psychotics as their condition deteriorates exactly resembles many of the so-called 'advanced' trends in official modern art. But it is clear that, far from being 'advanced' or 'progressive', such trends in painting are regressive and primitive (hence the vogue for primitive art and 'naive' painters).

It seems that a similar pattern can be discerned in modern music. Here the traumatic irruption of technology is represented by the invention and widespread use of the phonograph. Prior to this the best music was the almost exclusive possession of a cultured leisure-class who patronized composers, attended their concerts and operas, and performed their works at home. But with the coming of the gramophone record at prices anyone could afford, all this changed. Now anyone could listen to Beethoven quartets at home without the rather considerable expense of hiring four musicians to play them (or, alternatively, without having to study music for long enough to be able to perform them with similarly qualified friends). Now the intellectual, cultured music of the elite become accessible to everyone and was no longer the secure and exclusive possession of a superior class.

Consequently, some composers, who considered themselves to be particularly cultured, exclusive and elitist began to write music which, even allowing for the gramophone record, would still be appreciated by only a tiny minority of true *savants* and initiates. Hence melody and rhythm immediately began to give way to increasingly amorphous and abstract music in which tunes as such seldom if ever emerge and in which the beat is not continued beyond a few bars before being changed. Such music de-emphasizes sensual and appealing qualities and sabotages ordinary harmony by seldom resolving anything into its home key; it submerges everything in a chromatic indefiniteness which makes listening hard going and appreciation difficult or impossible. Indeed, the Second Viennese School eventually abandoned the diatonic system altogether in favour of keyless 'twelve-tone rows'; while other tendencies in so-called *avant-garde* music substitute noises for notes, or even, in the case of one of John Cage's works, total silence for sound itself. Such a development is exactly parallel to the case of modern painting, and in both instances total negativism and gross irrationality seem to have been the outcome.

Of course, this process of withdrawal from the real world has an exact and revealing parallel in the psychoses; indeed, it is in many ways the essential psychotic symptom. For if, as we have already seen, the psychoses can be represented as a conflict between the ego and reality, then a withdrawal from, and abandonment of, that reality is an obvious outcome if that conflict cannot be resolved. Thus there is a similarity between madness and modernity in art, not merely in outward forms of expression, but in inner logic and fundamental psychology. Along with the other externalizations of psychopathology discussed above, modern art has become increasingly an externalisation of the psychoses, and of these perhaps most especially the more schizoid forms. So obvious is this in the case of Surrealism that it hardly calls for comment; here, undeniably, is a movement dedicated to the externalization and realization of insanity as art!

Surrealism was in large part a literary movement, but in much of modern literature as a whole I believe that we can discern a conflict between artistic narcissism and modern progress comparable to that which we have already found in the cases of painting and music. Here the cause must lie in the social, commercial and educational advances which made literacy practically universal and books both cheap and easily obtainable. Once again, as in music and painting, there is a tendency to make serious literature as difficult as possible and demanding of a subjective attitude on the part of the reader which will define him as educated and 'sensitive'. While the masses read cheap novels with strong story-lines, obvious characters and definite endings, the 'serious' writer increasingly produces works which negate all these tendencies. Story-lines become involved and perverse, if not absent altogether in some cases; characters become increasingly uncommon and eccentric, and themes unacceptable to the masses such as suicide, homosexuality, alienation, despair, madness and meaninglessness become increasingly popular in 'advanced' fiction. The hero or the happy ending goes out of fashion because it has become too trite — that is, too close to popular style.

In especially acute cases language itself undergoes changes exactly comparable to those seen in schizophrenia where the degradation of speech occurs in a number of characteristic ways. One quite common tendency is to form neologisms — in effect, to begin to create a private language, something obviously related to the state of narcissistic withdrawal which underlies the disease. Words like 'superskeletonization' appeared in the speech of one schizophrenic with a *penchant* for lengthy neologisms. His

Art, Externalization and Insight

longest word consisted of a full fifty letters: 'semicentiosteophotoseismophysiopleopolycomputation'![1]
I do not know whether a neologistic schizophrenic has ever tried to write a novel, but if he did it might well closely resemble one of the alleged masterpieces of modern English literature, James Joyce's *Finnegan's Wake* — a piece of fiction written in a private Anglo-Irish *patois* which is nothing if not neologistic and which, in its third paragraph, contains a neologism even longer than that just quoted:

> The fall (bababadalgharaghtakamminarronnkonnbronntonnerronntuonnthuntrovarrhounawnskawntoohoohoordenenthurnuk!) of a once wallstrait oldparr is retaled early in bed and later on life down through all Christian minstrelsy. The great fall of the offwall entailed at such short notice the pftjschute of Finnegan, erse solid man, that the humptyhillhead of humself promptly sends an unquiring one well to the west in quest of his tumptytumtoes: and their upturnpikepointandplace is at the knock out in the park where oranges have been laid to rust upon the green since devlinsfirst loved livvy.

Another tendency in the language of schizophrenics is towards so-called 'word-salad', a disorder in which most grammatical structure disappears to produce an irrational telegraphic style of utterance, often almost totally lacking in sustained sense:

> Do I see cake Do I do the reverse of acting
> Yes Do I feel sensually deceived
> thoughts in mental suggestion in increase of
> senses in suggestion
> senses deceptive

---

[1] S. Arieti, *The Interpretation of Schizophrenia*, London, 1974, p. 266.

in in deception deception deception deception[2]

Contrast this schizophrenic word-salad with the following quotation from Samuel Beckett's punctuationless novel, *How It Is*:

> my life a voice without quaqua on all sides words scraps then nothing then again more words more scraps the same ill-spoken ill-heard then nothing not stretch of time then in me in the vault bone-white if there were a light bits and scraps ten seconds fifteen seconds ill-heard ill-remembered ill-heard ill-recorded my whole life gibberish garbled sixfold[3]

— a judgement with which some might well not wish to disagree.

Again, schizophrenic speech is often derailed and disturbed by chance associations of sound and meaning which conspire to produce rhyming or alliterative effects with frequent repetition and little apparent sense:

> Look Up The Word Passions In The Encyclopedia
> (A Masterpiece Of A Word) And In The Dictionaries.
> Don't Get Cerebral Meningitis In Your Studies
>   But You Will Find That There Is A Difference
> Between The Passions of Jesus of Bethlehem And
> The Passions Of Blue Beard
>   Between The Passion Of Misplaced Sympathies And
> The Passions Of Suicidal Thoughts.
>   Are You Passionately In Sympathy With Your Great
> Poet Dante, Doctor Arieti?
>   And I Am In Passionate Admiration Of The Works of
> Molière, The French Troubadour.

---

[2] *Ibid.*, p. 265
[3] *Ibid.*, p. 146.

Art, Externalization and Insight

And There Is The Passion Flower
And The Passion Plays Of Oberammergau.[4]

Compare this piece by a patient of Arieti's with the following quotation from Ionesco's *The Bald Prima Donna*:

Mr Smith: The dogs have got fleas, the dogs have got fleas.
Mrs Martin: Cock fowl duck, cock fowl duck, cock fowl duck.
Mrs Smith: Cock, you're fowling us.
Mr Martin: I'd rather lay an egg than steal an ox.
Mr Smith: Mucky duck!
Mrs Martin: [. . .] Ah! Oh! Ah! Oh! Stop grinding my teeth!
Mr Smith: Your eyes are putrefying.
Mr Martin: Let's go and slap Ulysses.
Mr Smith: I'm off to my little hut in Cockaigne.
Mrs Martin: The cockatoos of Cockaigne have cockeyed cockscombs! The cockatoos of Cockaigne have cockeyed cockscombes! The cockatoos of Cockaigne have cockeyed cockscombes!
Mrs Smith: The mice have got lice, the lice haven't got mice.

(Following which, I think, the observation that there is also the Passion Play of Oberammergau seems strangely apt.)

Admittedly, not all modern artists, writers and composers have been equally prone to such pathological tendencies; but it remains a fact that nearly every one who has aspired to be considered *avant-garde* has committed such absurdities to some extent, and many to a great extent. No one, I think, could claim that Impressionism, Cubism, Surrealism and so on were not central schools of modern painting; and atonality, rhythmic complexity and formal

[4] *Ibid.*, p. 260.

arbitrariness can hardly be called atypical features of modern music. Some of the works of writers like Beckett, Joyce and Ionesco may represent extremes even in modern literature, but these authors could not be described as eccentric, peripheral or without influence. Most readers will agree that the features of modernism in the arts which I have picked out are not inessential ones and that they do call for comment. It has for a long time been a commonplace among *avant-garde* connoisseurs to castigate the philistine man in the street for his uncomprehending dismissal of most of modern art as a species of insanity, but on this occasion the man in the street — who, unlike the connoisseurs, is not defending a vested, or *invested*, interest — might just be right.

If we ask ourselves why it is in the field of art and literature most particularly that symptoms of a schizoid, psychotic conflict with reality have been most prominent, the answer is probably to be found in two principal considerations. First, there is the point that the impact of modern, scientific and technological culture was bound to be hardest on those with artistic, intuitive temperaments who expressed themselves through traditional, craft-like techniques. Second, there is the consideration that art and literature, perhaps more than anything else except religion, provide for a culturally-approved externalization of the unconscious and perhaps even more than religion, for the individual unconscious in particular. Hence, when the impact came, it registered strongly in fields of endeavour which were particularly vulnerable and particularly well suited for the expression of a psychological reaction very closely comparable to that of individual psychosis.

If the foregoing analysis of modern *avant-garde* artistic culture is at all correct, then it is significant in drawing attention to the basic causal factor in the situation — that is, the traumatic intrusion of modernity into otherwise traditional fields of expression. It seems likely that such is also the case where some other pathological aspects of modern culture are concerned, including the failures in individual ego- and superego-development to which I have already drawn the reader's attention. In this case too, problems have arisen because of traumatic intrusions of modernity, mainly in the form of scientific and social developments which have undermined one of the most important cultural factors of all — religion.

We saw earlier that the principal consequence of the primal trauma was the creation of religious rituals concerned with initiation and totemism which acted as cultural means of maintaining the repressions, sublimations and prohibitions on which civilization had to be based. But we also saw that with the coming of agriculture the old totemic religion became increasingly irrelevant and that the return to something like the original grain-eating economy with its primal horde-like divine monarchies endangered the co-operative altruism on which the hunting economy had been based and carried the real possibility of a break-down in internal restraint and its replacement by external coercion. In fact, the latter seems to have occurred in the divine monarchies which evolved into welfare state totalitarianisms and, as we can see, something like this may be happening today. But, as in the Neolithic, the cause of our cultural problem lies in an economic and technological revolution — one which, in its scale and importance is only comparable with the Neolithic — which has had the inevitable consequence of undermining traditional religious and cultural values and thereby has jeopardized those delicate structures of repression, inhibition and sublimation on which all cultures depend. In the study of modern psychopathology from which I have quoted so many times already we find an explicit and particular expression of this general point:

The generation of fathers who drew their standards from religion, thus speaking in the name of divine laws, possessed an entirely different strength in the education of their offspring from the following generation. It was also easier for their child to bear the religiously founded superego, by which the father made his demands not only out of his own choice but in the name of a higher being to whom he had to submit as the child had to submit to him. A generation which follows a religious one still develops a superego deriving its strength from the identification with the unshaken father. Thus Freud (and his generation) could say: 'Morality is always a matter of course'. This saying seems to have lost its validity today.

In former times parents considered it their task to teach children moral values. Although infantile sexuality was not consciously perceived and therefore denied, nevertheless the child was considered impulsive and unbridled; the educational task consisted in changing the child from a savage into a valuable member of civilized society. Upbringing was a positive task. In recent decades parents and educators, insecure in this task, have been mainly afraid of harming the next generation and of losing its love.[5]

As I have already remarked, the diffidence of parents and educators in inculcating moral values may in part be due to a mis-understanding of psychoanalysis brought about through excessive therapeutic concern and the individualistic fallacy (although another factor to be mentioned shortly could not have been unimportant); however, the principal cause of this decline in confidence in traditional standards is obviously the triumph of entirely novel authorities represented by modern science and technology. In large part, this has been responsible for the decay and collapse of traditional values. Just as the camera intruded into the world of the painter and brought with it technological development in the place of traditional skill,

[5] Lowenfeld, 'Our permissive society and the superego', pp. 606–7.

so science in the form, for instance, of modern cosmology or the theory of evolution, irrupted into the hitherto traditional field of religious dogma and denied long-established truths. Little wonder, then, that in time religion itself became suspect, and men and women have begun to look increasingly towards science and other modern sources for their values and beliefs.

Expressed in terms of ego-psychology, we might say that what has occurred is a traumatic intrusion of reality into previously secure superego-structures and ego-defences. In the case of the modern arts, technological innovations disturbed the traditional relationship between many artists' egos and the reality they sought to depict. The result, as we saw, was a turning away from reality, but also a consequential regression in the ego itself expressed in the increasingly primitive, fragmented and withdrawn style of modern artistic expression.

If we ask ourselves why this should be so — because, on the face of it, there seems no obvious reason why a turning away from reality should necessarily imply any degradation in the ego — we can perhaps explain it by recalling the discussion of the nature of the ego offered earlier. We saw that, above all, the ego was charged with responsibility for the management of voluntary movement which, in a creature provided with relatively unfocused, diffuse drives rather than automatic, exact instinctual responses, also implies control and direction of those drives through the use of higher mental functions of reality-testing, choice between alternatives and, above all, rationality. While the id is dominated by the pleasure principle — namely, a need to find satisfaction for its internal instinctual excitations — the ego, by contrast, has in part at least to recognize the demands of reality, even when planning purely instinctual gratification. Because information from the senses is essential for voluntary movement the ego cannot ignore the reality which those senses depict. Still less can it ignore those other sensations which come to it from inside the organism: subjective sensations which we call the emotions, intuitions, wishes and trains of thought which arise spontaneously out of the unconscious and which are the ego's principal means of sensing the force and direction of the drives of the id. Thus if the ego turns away from both inner and outer reality and denies or ignores the evidence of sensation it is improverishing itself and behaving like some isolated dictator who, because he trusts and respects no one, fails to receive the information, advice and intelligence on which all effective political action depends. In a way which is all too familiar to us from historical examples, he is likely to isolate himself and lose contact with the very reality on which his position as leader depends. Insulated from reality by his own arrogance and the sycophancy of his retinue, he is likely to be the last to realize what is happening when the revolution finally comes. An analogous fate can befall the ego if, in its psychic functions of government of the mind and body, it fails to heed the annoying, but important, intrusions of reality represented by the evidence of the senses, subjective feeling and its acquired capacity for self-judgement. As it turns away from these, so it loses its essential minimal commitment to the reality principle and becomes progressively subject to the pleasure principle and the wishes of the id. Expressed in structural terms, one can say that it does indeed begin to undergo regression, beginning to dissolve back into the id from which it originally emerged.

In this discussion the process of externalization should not be confused with the operation of the reality principle. Far from resulting in the ego's true acceptance of reality, externalization of the kind we have seen in modern art, acted-out Oedipal conflicts, or drug-dependency, produces the exactly opposite effect. This is because the externalization is defensive; its aim is to save the ego the unpleasant necessity of recognizing disturbing conflicts within its own house by promoting the fiction that they occur only outside it. Here, assuredly, the conflict may be taken very seriously — often more seriously than the objective conditions dictate — but it is never taken seriously as an internal, subjective one for which purely external remedies are unlikely to be effective. The net result is not the recognition of an internal conflict clearly perceived in objective terms, but rather an objective conflict completely misconceived in subjective terms. In short, the fact that the paranoiac believes that his delusions are real does not save him from losing contact with reality; on the contrary, it makes it inevitable.

This, then, is why modern art in particular, and many aspects of modern culture in general, represent the progressive degradation of ego — and superego - functions such as realism, intelligence, rational coherence, control and the capacity for instinctual renunciation. It is the essential reason why modern art in particular and culture in general seems to be increasingly dominated by trends more compatible with the id than the ego — namely, those that demand instinctual gratification at more or less any cost and are characterized by irrationality, ambivalence, incoherence, phantasy and primitive indentifications.

In this process of regression and ego-degradation it seems that the last-acquired and most elaborate structure within the ego organization, the superego, was the first casualty. When our perception of reality became incompatible with our cultural superego-structures in the form of the conflict of modern science and society with religion, the superego began to give way. This, in itself, was not an undesirable or necessarily pathological phenomenon. The superego, a split-off and frequently oppressive institution within the personality, stood in many ways in relation to it as the ego itself stood to the id — a distinguishable entity in itself, largely unconscious, and sometimes making demands on the ego which could lead to severe and unnecessary inner conflict. Yet the erosion of the superego also posed a great threat and danger to the ego, because there was no way of being sure that in every case where a dissolution of the superego took place a corresponding enlargement of the ego would follow.

The fact seems to be that the superego is something which is most essential to both the individual and the culture in their early evolutionary states. The child needs the institution of the superego because the only certain way that his ego can master its perverse and anti-social instinctual drives is by some measure of internalization of the image, prohibitions and moral authority of the parents. Nowhere have I found this vitally important, but frequently ignored, point better expressed than in a characteristically flamboyant, but also characteristically penetrating, flight of rhetoric by Salvador Dali, a modern artist who has combined unparalleled externalization of madness with considerable intuitive insight into it. Speaking of his father, 'a giant of strength, violence, authority, and imperious love. Moses plus Jupiter', he says.

> In order for me to become Dali, I had to immolate on the psychoanalytical altar my father Dali y Cusi; shrink him as do the Java headhunters to the size of one of those celluloid toys that as a child I hammered to bits, and swallow him like the Euch aristic host so as to digest him and be nurtured by his substance and essence. For I must, at the same time, never cease to keep his admirable presence before me, so that my wild rage of power and resentment might not get the better of me, but remain channelized and mold itself little by little into the monumental projection that would be he and I, me and him, my genius flowering with the secret of his strength.[6]

In the evolution of culture, too, there seems no reason to

[6] *The Unspeakable Confessions of Salvador Dali*, London, 1976, p. 24.

doubt that the cultural, collective superego — in other words, religion — was an essential acquisition; and it is no accident that psychoanalytic studies of culture which do not fall prey to the individualistic fallacy should devote so much space to the religious question. It seems extremely likely that without the acquisition of the animal-phobic superego of totemism early hunter-gatherer societies could not have evolved or that late ones like those which covered the caves at Lascaux and elsewhere with totemic emblems could not have survived. Furthermore, we have already seen why it is that the superego-epiphanies of the primal father and mother were necessary in sustaining subsequent cultural developments such as agriculture and pastoralism.

Yet all these developments were, in part at least, at the expense of the ego in that they limited and confined it to the extent that they reinforced it. Like a plaster cast which encases a broken limb, the superego may have an essential role to play as long as the ego itself is unable to sustain itself unaided, but as soon as the limb is healed the cast becomes encumbering. By identifying himself with the father the child may be ensuring that his 'wild rage of power and resentment might not get the better of him' but, in adult life, when the ego should be competent to make its own decisions and control the id itself, the imposition of an alien ego — that of the father — may be less than beneficial. Indeed, as we have already seen, the more completely repressed, primitive parts of the superego may become especially maladaptive.

In the history of culture there is no doubt that the persistence of religion beyond its appropriate time and outside its essential sphere has caused inestimable suffering and problems for humanity. For instance, religion should never have been allowed to cloud man's scientific awareness of himself and the world around him, yet, demonstrably, religious institutions like the Holy Roman Inquisition, or superego institutions like the phantasy of a personal creator God have done immeasurable harm in bringing about the suppression of the scientific insights of men like Darwin and Galileo — not to mention Freud. The question of the role of the superego in childhood and adult life largely boils down to the question of *insight*. It is probably not fortuitous that the problem of insight has begun to engage the attention of psychoanalysts of late[7] or that it has been the subject of two recent papers by Anna Freud. Speaking as an analyst, Anna Freud remarks that 'we take it for granted that the amount of insight possessed by an unanalyzed person is minimal, and that this is due to the protective barrier between the id and the ego, erected to shield the latter from any excessive awareness of mental discomfort, pain, anxiety, narcissistic hurt, etc.'[8] She subtitles this paper 'Self-knowledge as the communication between the id and ego', and it is in this sense that insight achieves its fullest psychological meaning. Essentially, insight means the knowledge at the disposal of the ego regarding itself, the superego and the wholly unconscious id. Of course, direct, conscious knowledge of the latter is impossible because the unconscious is, by definition, unconscious. However, the ego can obtain extensive indirect knowledge of its id — not to mention the unconscious part of the superego — by undergoing a competently carried out psychoanalysis, or, in rather rare cases, through the possession of poetic or artistic gifts or an unusual capacity for candid self-knowledge.[9] But however it is acquired, insight never comes easily and can only be painfully wrested from the unconscious against the

---

[7] 'The decline in the appreciation of insight as the goal of psychoanalytic therapy has led to several recent efforts to re-establish its central role.' L. Rangell, 'Psychoanalysis and dynamic psychotherapy', *Psychoanalytic Quarterly*, L, no. 4 (1981), p. 679. See also H. P. Blum, 'The forbidden quest and the analytic ideal: the superego and insight', *ibid*.
[8] *Psychoanalytic Psychology of Normal Development*, London, 1982, p. 139.
[9] *Ibid*., pp. 147–8.

opposition of the force of resistance which tirelessly works to keep what is repressed away from all awareness of the ego.

In the infancy of society and culture, as in the analogous case of the infancy of the individual, insight has to remain severely limited because at this stage of psychological immmaturity the ego itself is severely restricted in its capacity both to control and to understand itself and the id. The consequence of neoteny in our species has been that we have become not merely foetalized in our adult anatomy and morphology, but also precociously sexually mature in our infancy in the sense that, as adults, we attain sexual maturity with bodies which are those of the immature young of our ancestors and with behavioural responses which are comparable. This immediately explains the playfulness, plasticity, perversity and general paedomorphic character of human sexual behaviour (in effect, another way of making the point about the diffusion of drives and the dominance of the cerebral cortex, itself, as was pointed out earlier, a neotenous phenomenon). Hence our species is typified by sexual foreplay and erotic activities of a notably child-like kind: embracing, holding hands and exchanging long, languid looks with the loved one, which reproduces behaviour otherwise only seen between mother and child; kissing, sucking and licking, which are obvious adult continuations of infantile suckling; manipulation of the genitals, and all manner of other activities normally labelled 'perverse', such as looking, showing, chastizing the buttocks, etc. All of these activities can be traced to infantile prototypes which, as psychoanalysis has demonstrated beyond any possible doubt, originate in childhood and owe their attraction to adults not merely because of early individual addiction to them but because of the species-wide neotenous trends in evolution which have made us child-like in form and somewhat infantile in sexual behaviour.

Such paedomorphic tendencies, while conductive to the evolution of the ego in that they have definitely established the cerebral cortex and with it the basic inhibitory functions of the mind, have not necessarily been equally conducive to the obtaining of insight in childhood. The lengthy immaturity of the human organism causes a considerable and, in most cases, permanent postponement of psychological maturity understood as a point where infantile ego-defences can be dismantled and mature management of the id take over. In the case of the species as a whole we saw much earlier what reasons there were for thinking that, had the original defences against the id and its drives not been unconscious and automatic, then the success of those defences might not have been at all long-lasting. Such automatic and unconscious defences against the id precluded much possibility of conscious insight since at that time, as is perhaps the situation in childhood, conscious recognition of the extent of the demands of the id would only have made resistance to them more difficult, and perhaps even impossible. Only when the ego has achieved some considerable measure of maturity and competence, and only when it has at its disposal a fully matured sexual apparatus is it in a position to make the transition to conscious, rational management of the id in place of unconscious, irrational defence. The former was not obtainable in the primal epoch of human culture, and the latter is unobtainable until adolescence in modern individuals. In both cases, then, postponement of the possibility of insight is the inevitable result.

Returning now from this short digression into the psychoanalytic meaning of insight, we can, I think, readily see that certain aspects of superego-erosion are not necessarily bad if that erosion leads to real insight and the concomitant enlargement of the ego. It was, in itself, no bad thing that Copernicus and Galileo showed that the earth had not been placed at the centre of the universe. In this case part of the collective neurosis — established religion — was wrested from the world of phantasy and replaced by insight into reality immeasurably more valuable in objective terms than the myth it replaced. Similarly, in individual cases, it is no bad thing when psychoanalysis reveals an unconscious burden of guilt and enables the individual to substitute for it rational, real perceptions of right and wrong. In both these examples the superego has been eroded and insight gained. But erosion of the superego — or, more seriously perhaps, of the ego itself — without insight is a pathological process which may well leave the individual or the socievy in which it occurs considerably worse off than before. To revert to my earlier analogy, it might be like throwing off the plaster cast before the limb was fully healed. In this event, only evil can result.

In my view this is precisely what has come about in the modern arts in particular and is increasingly coming about in modern culture and society in general. The old, outdated and superannuated superego-structures of traditionalism of all kinds have come crashing down around us under the onslaught of modernity. The result, as we have already seen in the case of the modern arts, has not always been the acceptance of reality and the winning of insight. On the contrary, a vertible flight from reality, diagnostically comparable to that of psychosis, is often the outcome. The externalization of neurotic, depressive and psychotic conflicts, which seems to have been one of the principal effects of the collapse of the superego in both the individual and the culture, has positively militated against the acquisition of any kind of insight both by presenting the illusion that these conflicts are autonomous and objective and by encouraging the belief that they can be remedied by purely external, tangible means. The growth of holistic, anti-psychological paradigms in the social sciences has only compounded this trend and complicated the problem by providing all-too-easy rationalizations for the externalization of conflicts whose true understanding can only be achieved through genuine insight.

The insights to which I am alluding here are inner, psychological ones; but these, no less than the objective realities, have vanished perhaps even more rapidly from modern art, literature and culture in general. K. R. Eissler observes, I think rightly, that

> During the course of the eighteenth century, Western man woke up to the perception, discernment and enjoyment of psychological subtlety and refinement such as the world had not known before . . . . The exquisite enlargement of responsiveness to human emotionality and detail . . . became explicit in the great psychological novels of nineteenth-century France and Russia, concomitantly with the philosophies of Schopenhauer and Nietzsche . . .
>
> It could not fail to happen that the new psychological understanding of man that had already imbued music, art, lilterature and philosophy became the subject as well of scientific psychology. This was the accomplishment of Freud. Such eminence had to be followed, of course, by a decline. With Richard Strauss . . . music reflecting the human world vanished. The psychological novel found its last representative in Proust . . . Auguste Rodin . . . was the last sculptor of human woes, passions and felicities.
>
> What now dominates music, art and literature is dehumanized abstractions . . .[10]

Surveying modern artistic, literary and intellectual culture in general one gets the impression that, round about the time of the First World War, a great change came over Western man, a change which led him to turn away, perhaps decisively, from the great insights that had been accruing in every field of humanistic endeavour up to that

---

[10] *Talent and Genius*, New York, 1971, pp. vii–viii.

time. It is almost as if, brought to the rim of the great abyss of the human soul opened up by such geniuses of insight as Dostoevsky, Nietzsche and Freud, Western man backed cautiously away, unwilling or unable to fathom what lay before him. Since then, superficiality, banality and philistinism on a truly colossal scale seem to have become the order of the day. One wonders with what mixture of baffled amusement, contempt and incomprehension future generations will meet the artistic and intellectual wonders of the twentieth century! They will probably conclude — perhaps rightly — that most of us must have been either fools or madmen.

Less vehemently, perhaps, they will probably be right to conclude that the fundamental pathological trend of modern culture was one of superego-degradation without gain in insight or corresponding enlargement in the ego but, on the contrary, some degree of degradation in the ego itself expressed in increasing externalization of psychopathology, in a vast extention in the power of the state, and in psychotic tendencies in artistic expression.

Nevertheless, it would be a distortion of the truth to maintain that modern culture was in all respects dominated by a flight from inner and outer reality like that which we have seen in much of the modern arts. Not all modern artists and intellectuals have been guilty of the absurdities of so-called 'modernism', even if a large number of them have. There are undoubtedly some notable exceptions; and an example which might contrast rather effectively with the case of painting is provided by the cinema. Here, exactly the same technological development which triggered the flight from reality which we call 'modern' art produced the camera able to take moving pictures. Nevertheless, true to the principles which I argued were implicated in the modern arts' flight from reality, it is noteworthy that it was not those engaged in high-class, elite culture who made the early contributions to the development of the moving film, but rather actors, writers and directors who had originated in vaudeville and the popular theatre. For these people, undaunted by elitist — and therefore traditional — values, the technological development which enabled them to record their performances on the new medium of film represented an example of a welcome and indeed eagerly exploited advance. For them, by contrast to the so-called *avant-garde* of European painting, the camera created, rather than destroyed, an art form.

If we enquire into the response to the coming of photography in these two examples, it is not hard to see that the explanation lies in the differing interests and needs of the persons concerned. Some traditional painters found the invention of photography traumatic and responded to it by flight because it threatened — or, at least, seemed to threaten — their very *raison d'être* where the representation of appearances was concerned. The early cinema pioneers, however, coming from the world of mass popular entertainment where the size of the audience was the crucial factor in success, saw the new development as one which would open up the possibility of exponential increases in the number of spectators who could see each and every act that was recorded in the new medium. In this way a technological change which spelt disaster for many painters produced unequalled opportunity for many actors and entertainers.

This is a general principle which must apply to all technolocial and scientific advances: they benefit some who accept them eagerly; they harm others who oppose, deny or take flight from them. But it is also a principle which applies to scientific and other insights in general and, perhaps more especially, to the most important insights of all — those about ourselves and our societies. Externalization can, in certain very special circumstances, promote insight — for instance, in the course of the externalization of the patient's inner conflict, which comes about in the psychoanalytic transference[11] — but, as we have seen, in modern socieity as a whole its effect tends to be the exact opposite of this. In this case, externalization is a defence, not a stage on the road to self-mastery; it is a regressive phenomenon rather than the progressive one which it is made out to be. Thus with regard to advances in essential insight in modern society we can recast the general principle stated above in a more precise form: we can say that psychological and social insights will be accepted if they prove serviceable to externalization as a defensive, regressive force, but will be opposed if they come into conflict with it. Nowhere is this more clearly or more crucially seen than in the case of the source of the most profound insights of all — psychoanalysis itself.

It seems very clear that if we enquire into the fate of psychoanalysis in the twentieth century and the response that it has been accorded, two very different trends can be determined. To the extent that the teachings of Freud and of psychoanalysis in general could be represented as contributing to that revolt against boundaries and restraints which we noticed earlier, it was warmly welcomed and widely accepted, at least by those who identified themselves with the 'liberating' allegedly 'progressive' — but, in reality, regressive — trends in our culture. But to the extent that it taught other, less welcome truths, which actually contradicted the foregoing interpretation, then psychoanalysis was strongly and persistently resisted.

One of the clearest examples which one can cite of this is modern attitudes to sexuality. Psychoanalysis has certainly influenced these attitudes, but it is notable that its influence has mainly been interpreted as contributing to the assault

---

[11] Anna Freud, *Normality and Pathology in Childhood*, p. 42.

on sexual taboos and inhibitions. This has resulted in some welcome tendencies towards much greater candour and objectivity about sexual matters, but psychoanalysis can in no way be held responsible for the trivialization and debasement of sexuality which is now so apparent all around us. What psychoanlysis takes so seriously — indeed, what it makes in many respects one of the ultimate realities of human existence — modern 'sexologists' debase into something analogous to our appetite for food; they portray it as a diverting hobby, as a sport, or merely as a way of obtaining pleasure and relaxation. Of the profound psychological significance of each and every component of the sexual instinct and the awesome, but hard realities which it reflects, they say little or nothing. This thorough-going debasement of the significance of sexuality reflects a similar situation which we have already noticed with regard to it in childhood: modern sexual attitudes reflect a shift away from repression and denial of sex to its recognition and acceptance as nothing of any great importance, certainly as far the mind and the culture are concerned. Hence the ludicrous insistence on the purely physical aspects of sexuality and the almost total neglect of the unconscious, psychological ones; hence the continued unpopularity of the libido theory, and the truly monumental absurdity of a civilization that exploits sex with unparalleled vulgarity and tastelessness but which cannot recognize its immense significance in the symbolism of dreams, in the dynamics of personality or the foundations of culture. The shallowness of modern sexual freedom can hardly be underestimated; beneath it lies a prudery and denial of sexuality every bit as strong as that which modern, 'enlightened' opinion finds so objectionable in the Victorian era. The real difference is that we seek to neutralize and isolate sexuality from disturbing us by externalizing it as a trivial phenomenon, whereas our great-grandparents sought the same result through straightforward suppression. In that respect they were less hypocritical about it than we are.

Such a one-sided and biased interpretation of psychoanalysis was perhaps most understandable and least indefensible with regard to what we might call the first period of psychoanalytic research. This would run from the beginnings of psychoanalysis in the mid-1890s up until about 1920. This was the era of the discovery of the Freudian id and the invention and refinement of the classical technique of adult psychoanalysis. During this phase hysteria was a common disorder and obsessional neurosis became a paradigmatic Freudian neurosis.

The second period of psychoanalytic research runs from about 1920, and might be termed the era of the ego, if we describe the first as that of the id. Now the development of psychoanalytic ego-psycyology proceeded rapidly, marked by works like Freud's *Group Psychology and the Analysis of the Ego*, *The Ego and the Id*, and Anna Freud's *The Ego and the Mechanisms of Defence*. Writing in 1925, Freud could say that 'children have become the main subject of psychoanalytic research and have thus replaced in importance the neurotics on whom its studies began.'[12] Certainly, no one can deny that a great number of the analysts who rose to particular prominence between the 1920s and the present day have either been child-analysts themselves or have been influenced by those that were — the outstanding example, of course, being Anna Freud herself. During this phase of psychoanalysis, attention shifted, not just to children, but to the whole process of normal and pathological development, especially in relation to the ego and its defences. It also saw a notable increase in analytic interest in the pathology of the ego as evidenced, for instance, in the psychoses. In this phase it was more difficult, but still possible, to maintain the

---

[12] Preface to Aichhorn's *Wayward Youth*, XIX, p. 273.

fiction that psychoanalysis was a remissive, regressive doctrine aimed at freeing the instinctural drives of the id and nothing more. Increasingly clearly, psychoanalysis emerged as what it had always essentially been: a therapetutic technique and a scientific synthesis of insights in the service of the ego and its adjustment to itself, its id and to reality.

However, there is a possibility that a third phase of psychoanalytic research still lies in the future. As Freud himself pointed out, psychoanalysis might

> become indispensable to all the sciences which are concerned with the evolution of human civilization and its major institutions such as art, religion and the social order . . . The use of analysis for the treatment of the neuroses is only one of its applications; the future will perhaps show that it is not the most important one.[13]

If the first and second eras can be represented as those of the id and ego respectively, then this might well be that of the superego. In this phase attention would shift to culture as the chief subject of psychoanalytic research, just as it shifted from neurotics to children in the second. In part, this might be the consequence of advances in drug-therapy,[14] in part, of a process of externalization of psychopathology like that described above. If this were to come about, the great insights of the second era into individual child development might be complemented — perhaps in the way I have suggested in this book — by new researches into the origin and evolution of culture and its significance for individual development. In this third phase of psychoanalytic research the superego would be studied with an emphasis and detail comparable to that

[13] *The Question of Lay Analysis*, XX, p. 248.
[14] K. R. Eissler, 'Irreverent remarks about the present and future of psychoanalysis', p. 463.

which the ego received during the second, and applied psychoanalysis would at last come of age. With the super-ego, its values and its externalizations the whole domain of culture, civilization and society would come within the purview of a psychoanalysis which was now truly the science of man.

Such an outcome as this would do much to remedy the individualistic fallacy and correct the therapeutic tunnel-vision of many modern analysts; it would certainly make it very much more difficult to misrepresent psychoanalysis or use it to externalize psychopathology while suppressing insight. On the contrary, psychoanalysis would at last be in a position to describe and analyse such externalization, and perhaps even to point to some remedies. Much might be done to begin to reverse the present apparently inexorable drift towards ego- and superego-deterioration and the concomitant trend towards either anarchy or, more likely, tyranny. It is by no means far-fetched to think that psychoanalysis could bring about a new and original awareness of the significance of the cultural evolution of humanity for the developmental history of the modern individual, and with it a realization of the necessity and value of the superego both in childhood and culture. Once persuaded of the need for the individual to recapitulate in his own development the turning-points in that of the race and culture as a whole, parents and educators might rapidly regain a positive, constructive view of socialization and with it the moral authority that they currently seem to lack.

In these circumstances the pathological phenomenon of externalization about which I have spoken so much might take on quite new significance. It might become the occasion for a widespread acceptance of psychoanalytic insights into culture and society which would then make it less of a pathological symptom and more of a parallel to the process of externalization of inner conflict which routinely occurs in the analytic transference. Thus what the first epoch of psychoanalytic research procured for individual psychotherapy and the second obtained for the analysis of the child, the third might achieve for the culture as a whole.

According to orthodox psychoanalysis, at the beginning of an individual analysis

> a real [doctor-patient] relationship exists which gradually and increasingly becomes distorted through the addition of regressive libidinal and aggressive elements which are transferred from the past on to the person of the analyst, and . . . this continues until in the fully formed transference neurosis the realistic relationship is completely submerged under the irrealistic one.[15]

On the collective level, it would certainly be tempting to see the present proliferation of absurd, mendacious and bizarre myths about Freud as an equivalent of the 'irrealistic' phase of the transference described here. It may well be that as a cultural phenomenon the impact of psychoanalysis has been in some ways comparable to that of an individual analysis: liberating and externalizing the repressed and transforming the person of the analyst — in the cultural context, Freud himself — into a phantasied protagonist in the as yet unresolved inner conflicts of the patient. This would surely explain the immense popularity of the current mythology regarding Freud and the extraordinary selectiveness which makes people ready to discover, decry and deprecate the mote which is in Freud's eye while ignoring the beams which positively bristle from the eyes of brothers Jung, Adler[16] or — to give him thoroughly undeserved prominence — Tausk.[17]

[15] Anna Freud, *Normality and Pathology in Childhood*, pp. 36–7.
[16] W. Kaufmann, *Freud versus Adler and Jung* (vol. III, *Discovering the Mind*), New York, 1982.
[17] K. R. Eissler, *Talent and Genius: The Fictitious Case of Tausk contra Freud*, New York, 1971.

Art, Externalization and Insight

Why is it that sensationalized, sanctimonious innuendo circulates about Freud's relations with his sister-in-law while Jung's squalid, disreputable and indefensible sexual imbroglios — some with his patients — go largely unremarked? Why is it that critics ostensibly defending scientific rectitude fall with undisguised glee on every alleged contradiction, illogicality and non-sequitur in Freud's works, while ignoring the glaring incoherence and disorder which remains still in the much-edited and rewritten Adler, or the rampant mysticism and irrationality of Jung? Why, in so many recent biographies of Freud, do those in his circle who were at odds with him at one time or another shine with such refulgent virtue, while he himself, and those who stayed his friends, are systematically denigrated and de-valued? What may hopefully be an all-time low in objectivity about Freud was marked recently when a journalist — admittedly one better known for his credulity regarding the occult than his knowledge of Freud — accused him of 'wrecking and destroying those he suspected of harbouring disloyalty'. We are apparently expected to belive that

> Jung . . . came close to insanity after the break with Freud. Wilheim Reich had a nervous breakdown and contemplated suicide. Victor Tausk, one of his most brilliant disciples, both hanged and shot himself when Freud turned his back on him. Herbert Silberer reacted to a particular brutal 'dismissal' by hanging himself from the window bars and leaving a torch shining on his face, so that his wife could see him when she came in. The 'crime' of all these disciples was that they showed too much of a tendency to think for themselves.[18]

[18] Colin Wilson writing in *Now!*, 25 July 1980. Devastating refutations of such nonsense as this can be found in the works by Eissler and Kaufmann mentioned in notes 16 and 17 and, indirectly, but very interestingly, in Anna Freud's 'Personal memories of Ernest Jones', *Psychoanalytic Psychology of Normal Development*, pp. 346–53.

Who will explain to future generations why it was that in the twentieth century Jung's evident anti-Semitism and pro-nazi sympathies were excused while Freud — in plain contravention of the facts — was portrayed in the words of the author of the puerilities above as 'sinister'? May it not be that this was so because Freud, in parallel with the clinical example, became the inevitable focus for the 'regressive libidinal and agressive elements which are transferred from the past on to the person of the analyst'? The truth is that Freud, like the analyst of the full-blown transference neurosis is too important to us to be merely what he is, he must, for a while, be what we make him; and in that condition our picture of him reveals more about ourselves than it does about him. Like some sunken statue encrusted with barnacles and buried in silt, the true face of Freud awaits its eventual salvage from the muddy waters of modern mythology.

Recent centuries have seen the onset of a trauma in human affairs unprecedented since the Neolithic. Just as the economic revolutions represented by the coming of hunting, cultivation and pastoralism were all linked to psychological and social upheavals, so the coming of the modern, technological and scientific society has precipitated a major trauma. In part, as we have seen, this trauma is comparable to the Neolithic precedent, but in part it is unique. Its uniqueness lies in the fact that as Nietzsche so vividly realized, *God is dead*. The death of God goes far beyond the Neolithic precedent. There, assuredly, the head of the state became God, but religion as such lived on and magic and superstition proliferated. Today, the state itself may well be becoming God in some instances, but religion as a force is clearly spent, despite whatever revivals and reactions continue (God's hair and nails can be expected to continue to grow for a little while longer!). Such revivals will always be fundamentally and ineradicably reactionary because a modern, industrial society really has no choice but to take scientific insights very seriously and to set about the solution of its problems — which are increasingly caused by science and technology — with the only efficacious means: scientific and technological ones.

As we have seen, the psychological corollary of the death of God is dissolution of the superego, externalization of psychopathology and insanity art and literature and, increasingly, in culture as a whole. The only real solution to the problem is that suggested by the clinical parallel mentioned above. Following 'the fully formed transference neurosis' in which 'the realistic relationship' between analyst and analysand 'is completely submerged under the irrealistic one, . . . The former is expected to re-establish itself at the very end of treatment after the infantile elements have been detached from it by interpretation and after the transference phenomena have accomplished the task ascribed to them: to provide insight.'[19] In other words, there would have to be a resolution of the collective transference which our culture has formed to psychoanalysis in general and the person of Freud in particular, culminating, as it would have to do, in the acquisition of collective insight. Yet here the clinical analogy appears to begin to break down because it will probably forever be impossible to provide psychoanalysis on a mass scale and with it any degree of widespread personal insight. Yet we should not despair; alternatives do exist which have well authenticated historical precedents.

At present, the crisis in our culture is to be explained by the fact that the trauma of the death of God and the concomitant collapse of all traditional authorities is being played out in the adult lives of individuals who have not been prepared for it in their childhood and adolescence.

---

[19] Anna Freud, *Normality and Pathology in Childhood*, p. 37.

We are in a crisis comparable to that which occurred when the first hominids began to hunt and to kill the primal fathers. When the latter were finally gone, and when consequently the Oedipal conflict broke out between the sons and fathers of the hunting bands, initiation ritual was probably rapidly evolved to deal with the situation and to make a civilizing adult trauma of rape and murder with its resultant guilt and remorse into a socializing adolescent one of ritual punishment for the same crimes. Later, when weaning and toilet-training became established as socializing processes in infancy, Oedipal socialization also shifted into childhood (accompanied in some cases by circumcision).

Today, a new and in many ways unprecedented trauma of incalculable consequences has broken on the human race. It is a trauma caused by the immense irruption of scientific insights and technological innovations into every sphere of life. It is a trauma which has weakened and perhaps destroyed the sources of religion, and has eroded the superego to a dangerous degree. As long as it is a trauma which is mainly experienced in adult life, its effects on the young are bound to be catastrophic, with consequences which we have already reviewed.

Yet there is no reason why this developmental trauma, like the three that preceded it, should not be integrated into the pattern of normal socialization and psycho-sexual development. Just as resolution of the Oedipal conflict was incorporated first into adolescence, then into childhood, and weaning and toilet-training became important elements in the oral and anal periods, so there is every reason to suppose that our modern cultural trauma — the dissolution of the superego — can be similarly integrated.

Earlier, I pointed out that the time-table and sequence of the recapitulation of the three previous cultural traumas in childhood were determined largely by the id: oral, anal and phallic stages became fixed as occasions for weaning, toilet-training and Oedipal resolution in a manner which we have since come to regard as normal. Yet a fourth stage of development exists which, both from the view of the ego and the id, is ideally pre-adapted to a personal recapitulation of our current cultural crisis — the genital phase. This is ushered in by puberty and should ideally culminate in maturity. An important element in normal maturing is the substitution of increasingly competent ego-controls for superego complusions and a large measure of emancipation, both from the persons of the parents, and their internal representations. This is an exact, internalized equivalent of the cultural crisis of modern times and, in *The Psychoanalysis of Culture*, I used the analogy of individual maturation to illustrate it. Yet the converse is also true. If modern times should signal the beginning of the maturity of the human reace, then the beginning of maturity in the individual should be the psychological equivalent of modern times.

Because the modern cultural crisis is the outcome of the acquisition of *insights* — insights which, whether welcomed or rejected, showed that God was dead — its only solution lies in integrating those insights into the pattern of normal development and thereby making the curtailment of the superego which normally occurs during the genital phase the occasion for a corresponding enhancement of the ego which only the acquisition of such insights can procure.

Of course, this cannot take place without the initial normal development of the superego necessary for successful resolution of the three preceding stages, especially the phallic one. It is in general true that the adult ego has little hope of mastering the instinctual drives of its id if the superego has not been able to master them in childhood. Thus a superego must first be properly consistuted before its more rational and mature elements can be taken over into the ego, and its more irrational and primitive ones superseded. This substitution of ego for superego and its mastery of the id is the modern psychoanalytic equivalent of Nietzsche's reaction to the death of God — the need for the *Übermensch*, the man who has overcome himself. Such self-mastery is the quintessence of maturity.

Yet how is such a thing to come about in the absence of universal adolescent psychoanalysis? Principally, by two means. First, I see no reason why the later years of secondary, or the first years of tertiary education should not be in part devoted to giving young people insight into themselves through sensitive education in basic psychoanalytic psychology, even if individual analysis is not possible. Such educational programmes, aimed at providing true insight, might do much to ease the problems of adolescence and to pave the way for a more normal and healthy childhood for future generations. They could most certainly not be worse than what is provided in this respect at present — namely, nothing.

Second, it is important to avoid the common error of imagining that individual therapy can solve a collective, cultural problem. This is just another manifestation of the individualistic fallacy — a fallacy which fundamentally is itself only another example of resistance to psychoanalytic insight. Whilst it would be wrong to claim that only Freud's cultural insights and those relating to the value and necessity of the superego and instinctual restraint were resisted in modern culture, there is, as we have already seen, a great deal of truth in the assertion that psychoanalysis is only generally accepted if it can be put to use by the id and in the service of the pleasure principle, but that it will be resisted in so far as it serves its true interests: those of the ego and reality. Thus it is no accident that the individualistic fallacy and what I have called 'therapeutic tunnel-vision' have emerged along with other prejudices to maintain resistance to Freud's most precious insights — those into culture, the positive value of the

Art, Externalization and Insight

superego, and the necessity of instinctual renunciation and adherence to the reality principle. As we noticed earlier, all of these insights are missing, for instance, in the modern 'liberated' view of sexuality — a view that Freud may indeed have influenced, but which is not that of psychoanalysis.

Resistance to the cultural insights of psychoanlysis will obviously prevent any realization or acceptance of the realities of our modern cultural dilemma. As long as psychoanalysis remains an individual therapy and nothing more it will be powerless to contribute its insights to the solution of the fundamental problems of modern society for, as we have seen, even individual psychopathology is becoming increasingly externalized and implicated in the wider, cultural and social context. Only if there is a new, third phase of psychoanalytic research into culture and the constitution of the superego like that which I mentioned earlier does our culture have any hope of even beginning to resolve its increasingly acute pathology — pathology that is no longer confined to the indivudal neuroses but which is increasingly becoming that of an entire civilization.

Of one thing we can be quite certain: that if individuals do not achieve the genuine freedom which the internalization of restraint produces then the alternative is most likely to be not merely dissolution of the superego but also increasing externalization of restraint brought about by agencies of social control. If the death of God does not occasion the final emancipation of the ego from dependency on him it will only lead to that ego becoming the victim of his last will and testament: the Kingdom of God without the divine king — in other words, the modern, bureaucratic welfare state.

Bibliography

Arieti, S. *Interpretation of Schizophrenia*, London, 1974.
Arlow, J. 'Anal sensations and feelings of persecution', *The Psychoanalytic Quarterly*, 18 (1949), pp 79–84.
Badcock, C. *Lèvi-Strauss*, London, 1975.
The Psychoanalysis of Culture, Oxford, 1980.
Baudin, L. *A Socialist Empire: The Incas of Peru*, Princeton, 1961.
Beckett, S. *How It Is*. London, 1964.
Bender, L. 'The anal component in persecutory delusions,' *The Psychoanalytic Review*, 21 (1934), pp 75–85.
Borneman E. *The Psychoanalysis of Money* New York, 1976.
Campanella, 'City of the sun', in H. Morley (ed.), *Ideal Common-wealths*, London, 1885.
Custance, J. *Wisdom, Madness and Folly*, London, 1951.
Dali, S. *The Unspeakable Confessions of Salvador Dali*, London, 1976.
Eissler, K.R., 'Irreverent remarks about the present and future of psychoanalysis', *International Journal of Psychoanalysis*, 50 (1969) pp. 461–71.
Talent and Genius: The Fictitious Case of Tausk contra Freud, New York, 1971.
'The fall of man', *Psychoanalytic Study of the Child*, 30 (1975) pp. 589–646.
Engle, B.S. 'Attis a study in castration', *The Psychoanalytic Review*, 25 (1936), pp. 363–72.
'The amazons in ancient Greece', *The Psychoanalytic Quarterly*, 11 (1942), pp. 512–54.

Bibliography

Fenichel, O. *The Psychoanalytic Theory of Neurosis*, London, 1946.
Frazer, J. *Adonis, Attis, Osiris*, Part IV, *The Golden Bough*, London, 1936.
Spirits of the Corn and Wild, Part V, *The Golden Bough*
Balder the Beautiful, Part VII, *The Golden Bough*.
Freud, A. *The Ego and the Mechnisms of Defence*, London, 1968.
Normality and Pathology in Childhood, London, 1966.
Psychoanalytic Psychology of Normal Development, London, 1982.
Freud, S. Letter 75 (Fliess Papers), *The Standard Edition of the Complete Psychological Works of Sigmund Freud*, 1, London, 1953–74.
Three Essays on the Theory of Sexuality, Standard Edition, 7.
'Notes upon a case of obsessional neurosis', *Standard Edition*, 10.
'On the universal tendency to debasement in the sphere of love', *Standard Edition*, 11.
'Psychoanalytic notes upon an autobiographical account of a case of paranoia', *Standard Edition*, 12.
Totem and Taboo, Standard Edition, 13.
'Mourning and melancholia', *Standard Edition*, 14.
Group Psychology and the Analysis of the Ego, Standard Edition, 18.
'Neurosis and psychosis', *Standard Edition*, 19.
'The economic problem of masochism', *Standard Edition*, 19.
Preface to Aichhorn's *Wayward Youth*, Standard Edition, 19.
An Autobiographical Study, Standard Edition, 20.
The Future of An Illusion, Standard Edition, 21.
New Introductory Lectures on Psychoanalysis, Standard Edition, 22.
Friedman, M. and R. *Free to Choose*, Harmondsworth, 1980.
Hawkes J. and Woolley, L, *The History of Mankind*, New York, 1963.
Ionesco, E. *The Bald Prime Donna*, London, 1957.
Jolly, C. 'The seed-eaters: a new model of hominid differentiation based on a baboon analogy', *Man*, 5 (1970) pp. 5–25.
Jones, E. *The Life and Work of Sigmund Freud*, New York, 1953–57.

Bibliography

Joyce, J. *Finnegan's Wake*, London, 1961.
Kaufmann, W. *Freud versus Adler and Jung*, (*Discovering the Mind*, III), New York, 1982.
Lowenfeld, H. and Y. 'Our permissive society and the superego', *The Psychoanalytic Quarterly*, 39 (1970), pp. 590–608.
Martin, B. *A Sociology of Contemporary Cultural Change*, Oxford, 1981.
Neumann, E. *The Great Mother*, London 1955.
Niederland, W.G. 'Schreber's father', *Journal of the American Psychoanalytic Association*, 8, (1960), 492–9.
Pritchard, J.B. (Ed.), *Ancient Near-Eastern Texts Relating to the Old Testament*, Princeton, 1969.
Rado, S. 'The problem of melancholia', *International Journal of Psychoanalysis*, 9 (1928), 420–37.
Rangell, L. 'Psychoanalysis and dynamic psychotherapy', *The Psychoanalytic Quarterly*, 50 (1981) 665–93.
Reik, T. *Ritual*, New York, 1959.
Roheim, G. *Psychoanalysis and Anthropology*, New York, 1950.
Sandars, N.K. *The Epic of Gilgamesh*, Harmondsworth, 1980.
Shapiro, T. and Perry, R. 'Latency revisited' *Psychoanalytic Study of the Child*, 31 (1976), 79–105.
Staercke, A. 'The reversal of the libido sign in delusions of persecution', *International Journal of Psychoanalysis*, 1 (1920), 231–4.
Van Ophuijsen, J. 'On the origin of feelings of persecution', *International Journal of Psychoanalysis*, 1 (1920), 235–9.
Weigert-Vowinkel, E. 'The cult of the Magna Mater from the standpoint of psychoanalysis', *Psychiatry*, 1 (1938), 347–78.
Widengren, G. *The King and the Tree of Life in Ancient Near Eastern Religion*, Uppsala, 1951–54.
Woodburn, J. 'Hunters and gatherers today and reconstruction of the past', in E. Gellner, (ed.), *Soviet and Western Anthropology*, London, 1980.

Index

Abraham, Karl, 41
Abstractionism, 136, 137
Achilles, 50
Adler, 164, 165
Adolescence, 30, 92, 168
Adonis, 44, 48
Agdistis, 48
Aggression, 10, 11, 15, 17, 18, 21, 80
Agriculture, 38–43, 44, 47, 48, 54, 58, 60, 77, 79, 82, 115, 116, 145
Akhenaten (Amenhotep IV) 53, 58
Alcoholic intoxication, 115, 118–20, 132
Altruism, 7, 15, 16, 24, 25, 30, 59, 62, 108, 145
Amarna Letters, The, 56
Amazons, 48–50
Ambivalence, 21–4, 25, 149
Anal Phase, 41, 76–87, 115, 168
Animal phobia, 81, 151
Archaic heritage, 29, 70
Art, 135–8, 143, 144, 146, 147, 148, 149, 155, 156
Attis, 43, 46, 47, 52
Australian aborigines, 29, 37, 39, 77, 83–5, 89, 91, 115–16
Avant-Garde, the, 136–44

Bald Prima Donna, The, 143

Beckett, S., 142, 144
Bellerophon, 49
Brain, 2–5, 15, 32–4
Burial, 79

Cage, J., 139
Campanella, 117
Cerebral cortex, 3, 4, 5, 154
Cézanne, P., 136
Child-rearing
  and weaning, 39–42, 49
  and masculine mothers, 43–7
  and evolution of states, 60–1
  in modern world, 63–9, 90–4, 106, 131
  and social psychoanalysis, 72, 91
  in total societies, 111
  Schreber case, 122–3
Chimpanzee, 2–6, 7, 8, 14
Christ, 44, 46, 48
Christianity, 40–1, 44
Cinema, 157–8
Circumcision, 30, 168
City of the Sun, 117
Civilization, 14, 15, 17, 31, 68, 93, 145, 171. *See also* Culture
Civilization and its Discontents, 14 & n. 10
Clausewitz, 101
Clinical psychoanalysis, 9, 72,

175

73–5, 87, 171
Comedy, 44–5
Consciousness, 1, 2, 12, 25–6
Copernicus, 154
Co-regency, 53
Cubism, 136, 143
Culture, 6, 7, 15, 17, 23, 27, 62, 81, 95–6, 133, 145, 149, 155, 156–8, 162
Cybele, 43, 46, 48, 52

Dali, Salvador, 150
Darwin, 1, 152
Defence, 20–4, 25–6, 27 & n. 15, 28, 148–9, 154
Delayed-return subsistence, 38–9, 58, 104
Delinquency, 90, 94, 95–6, 126, 129
Delusions of persecution, 126. *See also* Paranoia
Depression, 42–4, 54, 114, 116, 117, 118, 132
Diana of Ephesus, 41, 107
Diffusion of instinct, 2–7, 13, 17, 23, 76, 153
Divine kings, 45–8, 50–3, 59–60
Drama, 44
Drug-addition, 131–2, 148
Duchamp, Marcel, 172

Ego,
    evolution of, 1–27, 34
    and defence, 27–8, 161
    and neoteny, 32–4
    and object-loss, 42–5
    in mania, 51–3, 55
    in groups, 66
    and stages of development, 86–7
    in total societies, 112–24
    and psychopathology, 127–34
    in modern society, 147–52
    and insight, 152–3, 154–7, 162

    and psychoanalysis, 161–2, 163
Ego and the Id, The, 161
Ego and the Mechanisms of Defence, The, 161
Egoism, 10, 15, 18, 23
Ego psychology, 2–27, 88, 147. *See also* Ego.
Egypt, 44, 46, 53, 54
Einstein, 37
Eissler, K. R., 156
Engle, B. S., 48, 50
Enkidu, 47
Envy, 108
Epic of Gilgamesh, The, 46–8, 50
Equality, 107–8
Evolution,
    of the ego, 1–27
    of man, 1–27
    and individualistic fallacy, 69–72
    of society, 16–27, 28–33, 38–61, 70–2, 78–85, 166–71
    theory of, 147
Expressionism, 137
Expressive Revolution, the, 97
External coercion, 24, 59–60, 68, 110–14, 116–18, 119, 120, 145
Externalization, 19, 59–60, 94, 110–14, 117, 118–35, 140, 148–9, 155, 157, 158–9, 160, 162–71

Fauvism, 136, 137
Female figurines, 39–41
Fenichel, O., 131
Finnegan's Wake, 141
Fire-cults, 57–8
Foetalization, *see* Neoteny
Food-addicts, 131
Frazer, J., 57
Freud, Anna, 73, 152, 161
Freud, Sigmund,
    on erect posture in man, 14
    on feminine masochism, 15
    and *Totem and Taboo*, 19, 72–3

Index

on origin of culture, 19, 68
and archaic heritage, 29
on latency, 32–4
and polytrauma theory, 37–8
and *Mourning and Melancholia*, 42, 45, 117–19, 120, 121
on return of primal father, 46
and infantile sexuality, 63, 77
on culture, 68, 112
and social psychoanalysis, 72–4
on ego in groups, 87–8
on superego, 95, 105
on psychopathology, 127
on modern culture, 152, 164–6
and future of psychoanalysis, 162

Galileo, 152, 154
Gelada baboon, 7–11, 12, 13, 14, 20, 31
'Gelada complex', 11
Genital mutilation, 29, 43, 48
Genital Phase, 93, 169–70
Germany, 125–7
Gilgamesh, 46–8, 50, 56
Golden Bough, The, 57
Gorilla, 2, 8, 14
Greece, 44
Greek mythology, 48–50
Group psychology, 66
Group Psychology and the Analysis of the Ego, 66, 119, 161
Guilt, 24, 28

Hamadryas baboon, 12
Hand, 5–6, 13–14
Hera, 50
Heracles, 49–50, 56
Heroes, 49–53
Holistic fallacy, 69–70, 155–6
Hominids, 9–11, 12, 13, 14, 15, 16, 17, 18, 26, 52, 168
Homosexuality, 47, 53–8

Horus, 41
How It Is, 142
Human evolution, 1–27
Hunting, 15–19, 26, 29, 32, 39, 40, 59, 79
Hysteria, 63, 81, 94, 128, 133, 161

Id, 2, 7–8, 9, 11, 12, 14, 15, 17, 22, 23, 25, 26, 28, 33, 69, 86–7, 127, 147, 149, 152, 154, 161, 162, 169
Identification, 11–12, 19–24
Identification with the aggressor, 11–12, 20
Immediate-return subsistence, 38–9, 59, 104, 131
Impressionism, 135–7, 143
Incas, 51, 110–14, 116–18, 119, 120
Incest, 23, 59, 95
Incest-avoidance, 11, 23, 24, 29, 65, 69, 81, 84, 85, 95, 97
Individualistic fallacy, 69–75, 77, 78, 88, 94, 110, 146, 163, 170
Infantile sexuality, 63, 76–88
Initiation, 29–31, 32, 37, 60–1, 79, 84, 92, 168
Insight, 24, 28, 152–9, 162, 167, 169
Inquisition, the, 151
Instinctual drives, 2–12, 17, 22, 23, 33, 46, 65, 69, 76, 78, 86–7, 127, 148, 154
Instinctual renunciaton, 78, 149, 171
Intelligence, 4, 5, 33
Internalization of coercion, 19, 21–4, 29–31, 68, 150, 171
Interpretation of Dreams, The, 73
Ionesco, E., 143, 144
Ishtar, 47
Isis, 41

Jews, 126
Jolly, Clifford, 9, 12, 13
Joyce, James, 141, 144

Jung, 164, 165, 166

Kinship system, 24
Kleinian School, 87

Language, 12–13, 34, 140–3
Lascaux, 151
Latency period, 32–4, 78, 83, 85, 89–92
Libido theory, 160
Literature, 140–4, 156
London School of Economics, 97

Madonna and child, 40, 41, 44
Malevitch, K., 137
Mammals, 4
Mania, 44–6, 51–3, 54, 55, 66, 115, 118–20, 121, 132
Manic-depressive disorders, 40, 41, 45–6, 52, 55, 82, 114, 115, 121, 127, 130, 131
Manual dexterity, 13–14
Martin, Bernice, 96, 97
Masochism, 11–12, 15
May-poles, 48
Megalomania, 45–7, 54–5, 121, 122
Melanesia, 77
Mesopotamia, 44, 51
Modernity,
  and social order, 62
  and permissiveness, 63–8, 76, 90, 106, 110, 113, 131
  and psychotherapy, 73–5
  in arts, 135–44, 147
  and culture, 144–7, 149, 155–71
Money, 126
Monotheism, 37, 80, 82
Monotraumatic theory, 37–8, 81
Mother-goddess, 29–41, 43, 44, 47, 51, 104–7, 131
Mourning, 39–40, 44, 117–18, 129
'Mourning and Melancholia', 42, 45
Multi-male group, 10, 16–18

Music, 138–9, 143–4

National Socialism, 125–6
Neolithic, Neolithic Revolution, 40, 58, 79, 91, 104, 106, 107, 145, 166
Neologisms, 140–1
Neoteny, 31–4, 85, 153–4
Neumann, 47
Neurosis, 23, 25–7, 28, 94, 128, 130
New York Psychoanalytic Institute, 90, 91
Nietzsche, 157, 166, 170

Object-loss, 42–5, 80, 114
Obsessional neurosis, 82, 94, 161
Oedipus, 11, 25, 87
Oedipus complex, 11, 26, 65, 70, 71, 76, 81, 85, 90, 93, 94, 101, 103, 106
Omphale, 50
One-male group, 10, 15–18, 26.
  See also Primal Horde
Oral Phase, 41, 76–87, 92, 103–8, 115, 168
Organic repression, 14, 15
Osiris, 44, 46, 48

Painting, 135–8, 146–57, 158
Palaeolithic, 39, 41, 104, 106
Paranoia, 13, 53–8, 82, 122, 123, 124, 125, 133, 149
Parricide, 19, 21, 23, 28, 29, 59, 79, 81, 83, 84, 95–102
Pastoralism, 79–81
Permissiveness, 63–8, 76, 90, 106, 110, 113, 131
Peru, 51, 110–14, 116–18, 119, 120
Phallic Phase, 76–87, 93, 95, 103, 115, 168
Pharoahs, 46, 56
Photography, 135–8, 146, 157
Pietà, 44
Pius XII, 105

Index

Pleasure principle, 148, 170
Police, 98–9, 101
Polytheism, 37, 40, 79, 82
Polytraumatic theory, 37–8, 54, 70, 78, 81
Postponement of gratification, 40, 60, 80, 82, 110, 115–16
Primal father, 10–11, 15, 16, 17–24, 26, 30, 46–8, 51, 53, 56–7
Primal horde, 10, 15–18, 26, 53, 59, 145
Primal mother, 40–3, 47, 48, 51, 52, 54, 55
Projection, 54, 123, 125, 133
Psychoanalysis, 27–8, 63, 69–75, 130, 152–71
Psychoanalysis of Culture, The, 15, 45, 46, 53, 77, 169
Psychosis, 127, 133–4, 135, 138, 139–40, 144, 149, 155, 161. *See also* Paranoia, Schizophrenia
Psychotherapy, 69–75, 78, 130
Public benefactors, 108
Pyramid Texts, The, 46

Rado, Sandor, 40, 51, 53
Reality principle, 148, 171
Reconstruction in psychoanalysis, 104
Reik, Theodor, 29 & n. 16
Relativity, 37
Religion, 23, 29–31, 37, 72, 145–7, 151–2, 166, 168
Repression, 25–7, 28, 128, 145
Resistance, 27–8, 153, 159–60, 170
Roheim, Geza, 11 n. 5, 39, 77, 83
Russia, 125–7

Saturnalia, 119
Schizophrenia, 82, 133–4, 140–1, 144. *See also* Paranoia, Psychosis
Schreber, 122
Science, 146, 151–2, 154–5, 167, 168

Secondary sexual characteristics, 8–11, 12
Second Viennese School, 139
Self-consciousness, 1, 2, 12, 25
Sexual behaviour,
  of chimpanzee, 3, 5, 6
  of man, 9–12, 153
Sexual dimorphism, 8–11
Sexual 'liberation', 64–9, 76–7, 159–60, 171
Sexual rivalry, 10–11, 17–24, 30, 168
Sexual selection, 10
Sight, 4–5, 14
Smell, 5, 14–15
Social control, 18, 111, 116, 120, 125, 171
Social cooperation, 15–19, 24, 59
Social evolution, 12, 16–27, 28–33, 38–61, 70–2, 78–85, 166–71
Socialism, 114, 115, 117–18, 120, 125–7
Socialization, 6, 29–31, 60–1, 62, 76–87, 91–4, 106, 111, 163, 168
Social psychoanalysis, 71, 103–4
Somatic externalization, 130
Son-gods, 44, 50–3
Speech, 12–13, 34
Strachey, J., 72, 73
Student protest, 97, 99–101, 103
Sublimation, 25
Suckling, 39, 41, 42, 49, 51–2, 53, 83, 86, 153
Sun-god, 56–7
Superego,
  distinctive of man, 1
  evolution of, 12, 13, 15, 17–24
  and verbal commands, 13, 34
  inheritance of, 28–31
  in mania, 51–3, 55
  and external coercion, 60, 68
  in modern society, 64–9, 74, 90, 92–109, 128, 147, 149–51, 157
  in groups, 66

in child-development, 86–7
primitive aspects of, 105–9, 123, 126
in total states, 111–24
in psychopathology, 127
and insight, 154–5
and future of psychoanalysis, 162–3
and modernity, 169–70
Surrealism, 140, 143

Taboo, 22–4, 29, 64–5, 81, 84, 85
Talbot, Fox, 135
Tammuz, 44, 46, 48
Tausk, V., 164
Terrorism, 98
Theseus, 50
Toilet-training, 60, 79–80, 83–4, 168
Totalitarian states, 50–1, 109–27, 132, 157
Totem and Taboo, 19, 21, 36, 37, 70, 72–3, 81
Totemism, 23, 29, 37, 59, 81, 84, 145, 151
Tragedy, 44

Transference, 164, 166, 167
Traumatic origin of society, 26–7, 28, 29–30, 37–45, 78, 79, 81, 93, 145
Trees, 47–8

Unconscious, 24, 25, 26, 27, 148, 152, 154
Upright posture, 5, 13, 14, 15
Uruk, 46, 48

Venice, 62, 65, 74–5
Venus of Willendorf, 41, 107

Weaning, 39–42, 49, 51, 58, 59, 60, 79, 80, 82, 83, 84, 103, 104, 115, 131, 168
Weigert-Vowinkel, E., 41, 42, 43
Welfare state, 50–1, 60, 106–14, 119, 123, 171
Witchraft, 57–8
Woodburn, James, 38 n. 1
Word-salad, 141–2

Zeus, 48
Zoos, 3